SELF-CARE STRATEGIES FOR FAMILY CAREGIVERS

Self-care Strategies for Family Caregivers

Paula Forte

Copyright © 2019 by Paula Forte.

Library of Congress Control Number: 2019911342
ISBN: Hardcover   978-1-7960-5119-3
             Softcover   978-1-7960-5118-6
             eBook   978-1-7960-5117-9

All rights reserved. No part of this book may be reproduced or transmitted in any form or by any means, electronic or mechanical, including photocopying, recording, or by any information storage and retrieval system, without permission in writing from the copyright owner.

Any people depicted in stock imagery provided by Getty Images are models, and such images are being used for illustrative purposes only.
Certain stock imagery © Getty Images.

Print information available on the last page.

Rev. date: 08/07/2019

To order additional copies of this book, contact:
Xlibris
1-888-795-4274
www.Xlibris.com
Orders@Xlibris.com
797039

CONTENTS

Acknowledgements vii
Preface ix
Introduction xi
Prologue: My Story xvii

Chapter 1   Self-care Strategies for Your Physical Needs 1
Chapter 2   Self-care Strategies for your Emotional Needs 14
Chapter 3   Self-care Strategies for your Educational Needs 25
Chapter 4   Self-care Strategies for your Spiritual Needs 39
Chapter 5   Self-care Strategies for Getting through Grief 51

Epilogue: Your Story 61
References 69
Bibliography & Resources 73

Acknowledgements

"The rose distils a healing balm the beating pulse of pain to calm" – Thomas Moore

It took a year to write this book. It was a genuine labor of love. I hope you will find it full of hope and respect for caregivers like you, who may be feeling tired and discouraged by the stress and strain of the work you do, *your labor of love*. I hope you will find in its pages the help you need, the encouragement you deserve, an appreciation of your work, which is often misunderstood, and the strategies you need to take care of yourself with kindness and compassion. I hope you find it to be a healing balm that invites you to put yourself first in matters of health: body, mind, and spirit.

> *The place of true healing is a fierce place. It's a giant place. It's a place of monstrous beauty and endless dark and glimmering light. And you have to work really, really, really hard to get there, but you can do it."* -- Cheryl Strayed

I need to thank several people who helped me bring all these ideas to the printed page. First, Sayre Darling, who edited my words and listened to my heart. Also, my peer-readers who carefully reviewed the manuscript in an effort to make it more readable and real: Susan Schumacher, M.S.N, R.N., Geriatric CNS, and also my friend; Lynn Choromanski, Ph.D., R.N., CNM, an informatics scholar and also my friend; Sr. Patrick Murphy, a member of the Presentation Sisters of Aberdeen, South Dakota, and a dear family friend; Robyn Birkeland, Ph.D., Study Counselor, Families and LTC Projects in the School of Public Health, University of Minnesota; and Tamara L. Statz, M.A., L.M.F.T., Study Counselor, Families and LTC Projects, Division of Health Policy and Management, School of Public Health, University of Minnesota. I appreciate their thorough review, candid comments and generous input, some of which was used to truly improve and enhance the final text. Finally, I want to thank Ben Musburger, M.S., L.A.M.F.T., hospice manager for North Memorial Health, for his wise counsel on the section about grief, Ricka Kohnstamm, a colleague and mentor, who wrote the Preface and Jules, a family caregiver, for graciously sharing her story.

Preface

As a mother, daughter, daughter-in-law, wife, sister and integrative health coach, I am intimately familiar with the virtues of care-giving. In my family, stepping up to care for others is a given. I have cared for children with chronic conditions, for parents and siblings with chronic disease and cancer, and I have cared for people I love at the end of life. And yes, it can feel rewarding and honoring. But that is only part of the story, the part of the story that is socially acceptable to talk about.

What is harder to be honest about is the overwhelming exhaustion that is part and parcel of the caregiving marathon. It is not easy to admit "I have a headache that won't go away, I think I am too tired." Or "I am worried that the lump in my breast is caused by all of the stress I have experienced over these past two years…" or "I am angry and resent you for what this is doing to our family."

As a Ph.D. nurse with a 44-year nursing career, as well as over a decade of family caregiving, Paula Forte normalizes this strenuous journey with candor and humor. She speaks knowledgeably and frankly about the ongoing effects of overwhelming stress and explains why it is critical to reserve some of our energy to care for ourselves, even while we are focused on caring for others. Reading Paula's book is like sitting at the kitchen table of a favorite teacher, one who has lived the struggle and offers wise, unpretentious, specific and helpful reminders of what I may have forgotten along the way…

Self-care strategies for physical needs
Self-care strategies for emotional needs
Self-care strategies for educational needs
Self-care strategies for spiritual needs
And finally, self-care strategies for getting through grief.

Paula's book is the self-care template I will keep within reach as a gentle reminder that keeping my own oxygen mask on is a critical component of caretaking and can soften the strenuous journey.

Ricka Kohnstamm, M.A., NBC-HWC

Introduction

This book offers five areas of strategies for anyone serving as a family caregiver. It may be of value for the sandwich generation, those adults who are caught caring for children as well as elderly parents; for the spouse reeling from the responsibilities of caring for a partner who used to share the household load, for siblings trying to look after each other as aging creeps in; and, for anyone trying to provide for the physical, emotional and spiritual needs of others who can no longer care for themselves. The Self-care Strategy sets include:

1. Self-care Strategies for your Physical Needs
2. Self-care Strategies for your Emotional Needs
3. Self-care Strategies for your Educational Needs
4. Self-care Strategies for your Spiritual Needs
5. Self-care Strategies for Getting through Grief

Each of these areas deserves attention.

The literature is clear, family caregivers are rarely inclined to attend to their own needs. Twenty-five years ago, Connell (1994) asked family caregivers what changes the act of caregiving had made to their own health practices. Acton, in reporting on Connell's work wrote, "One-third of the participants reported that they ate less nutritiously, exercised less, and used more medications to promote sleep…40% reported that their health had declined due to fatigue since they began their caregiving duties" (Acton, 2002).

Entering the 21st century Donelan and her colleagues noted that "2001 marked the implementation of the Family Caregiver Support Act, one of the first new federal initiatives designed to expand services and assistance for family caregivers" (Donelan et al, 2002). Their work examined the responses of over 1000 caregivers in 1998 and drew this conclusion. "As our society encourages more care in non-institutional settings, the impact on quality of care must be considered, with particular attention to the burdens on caregivers who are themselves elderly, ill, or infirm and who need instruction, support, and assistance to perform tasks safely and correctly" (Donelan et al, 2002).

Deeken and his colleagues looked for tools to measure the burden of caring and in doing so evaluated 28 instruments worthy of employment but noted little real action on the part of government or health professionals to measure or help manage the stressors caregivers face. They admonish that these tools could inform the healthcare community "so that professionals will know when and how to intervene to assist the overly burdened caregivers of their patients" (Deeken, Taylor, Mangan, Yabroff & Ingham, 2003). Yet as recently as 2017, Dionne-Odom and his colleagues noted that a "significant proportion of caregivers simultaneously report low engagement in all forms of self-care practices, high depression and anxiety, and low [Health-Related Quality of Life] HRQoL mental health scores" (Dionne-Odom et al, 2017). Wittenberg and Prosser write,

> "Caregiving dynamics have implications for the care patients receive. Negative effects on caregivers' well-being can limit their ability to provide high-quality care, so it's in patients' best interest for caregivers to be healthy. As deleterious health effects from caregiving accumulate, caregivers may become patients themselves and enter the health care system. Recognition of the spillover effects of caregiving highlights the interaction

between patient outcomes and caregiver outcomes" (Wittenberg & Prosser, 2016).

In fact, the consequences of the additional emotional, social and physical stressors of caring for someone with Alzheimer's disease or related dementias (ADRD) have a higher rate of dying prior to their care recipients. In a recent article by Gaugler and colleagues at the University of Minnesota's School of Public Health noted, "eighteen percent of spouse ADRD caregivers died before their care recipients, and [the] spouse caregivers had a significantly lower risk of mortality than their husbands or wives with ADRD (Gaugler et al, 2018)."

As we head toward the third decade of this new century it is time caregivers simply had a handbook for their self-care. Experts have known for decades that this is needed but little is available to guide the family caregiver toward holistic health and self-care success.

Coming from a 44-year nursing background and a decade of family caregiving, I am qualified to offer some practical strategies for caregivers to apply so that their wellbeing is not compromised in providing for the care of others. And, so that those in our care may not be put at risk due to our lack of investment in ourselves.

I'm writing this book because I know the literature on family caregiving. I know the risks we caregivers face. The odds are stacked against us as we shoulder the burden to care for those we love through circumstances that change repeatedly and where it often seems no one understands; although, "approximately 43.5 million family caregivers provide unpaid care to an adult or child. About 34.2 million care for a family member over the age of 50" (Family Caregiver Alliance and AARP, 2015). "The average duration of a caregiver's role is 4 years. Only 30% of caregivers provide care for less than a year. 24% of caregivers provide care for more than 5 years. 15% of caregivers provide care for 10 or more years. Higher-hour caregivers are twice as likely to have been in their caregiving role for 10 years or more" (National Alliance for Caregiving and AARP 2015).

Family caregivers can be anyone who invests time to carry on their daily routines, as well as, the additional support that provides for the life and wellbeing of those who need care. That said, you do not need to be a blood relative of the care recipient to be a family caregiver. Family can mean family of origin as well as family of choice. This was certainly true during the AIDS epidemic of the 1980s when gay community members took care of each other out of both love and desperation when so many healthcare agencies would not or could not provide the services needed.

As a family caregiver, I've had to figure out what part I can do and what jobs I must relinquish to others. I've had to determine how I will keep my sanity and my sense of humor as the circumstances of our lives and relationship change. I've had to deal with the loneliness, the obvious progression of my husband's disease and the realization of the consequences that the disease progression may bring. None of this is easy. All this effort also requires self-care skills that go well beyond the skill set acquired to take care of a family member in need.

Self-care is not necessarily a skill set a nurse (or any other health professional) would have. We are well trained to care for others and many nurses are quite well conditioned to put the needs of their patients before their own basic self-care. The literature is replete with the physical and mental health challenges nurses face as a result of their shift work, overtime schedules and the often abusive power structures in which they work. That is not true of *every* nurse, and, I am finding it is changing more quickly among younger nurses who seem to have embraced work-life-balance in a meaningful way. These young people, mostly women, seek to balance their work and life pressures as they flex their work around the ever-changing needs they face in raising families and building a life outside of their workplace. I applaud this new way of being my young colleagues have learned and embraced – they are often my best teachers when it comes to self-care.

I am a member of the boomer generation born in the years 1946 to 1964. Much like the traditionalists or the silent generation before us, we are often characterized as people who live to work rather than work to live. For me, my identity has always been merged with my career choice. "I am what I do" was a mantra I learned early in life. Now, with some maturity on me, and having to be a caregiver within my own family, I am diligently incorporating healthy self-care skills into my life every day. I have a lot of catching up to do. I realize that the stress I encounter because of the caregiving demands I face means I must step-up my game to do more to maintain my health and wellbeing. I also recognize that self-care skills are not second nature to me or my generation, so I am learning new skills that I am happy to pass on to you, my fellow caregivers.

I trust you will find in these pages some recommendations and some tools you are ready to employ for your own self-care journey. Some people believe that to be attentive to self-care is a selfish activity and for that reason they avoid it. Yes, it is selfish, it is, by its very nature *self-centered*. But that is not a derogatory term when you realize that your very life depends on it. The quality and even the length of your own life depends on how well you can balance the self-care needs you recognize and the caregiving needs you manage daily. Caring for others, especially someone you love can consume your body, soul and spirit, if you let it. Learning the skills of self-care can preserve your wellbeing in spite of the daily challenges you continually face in your family caregiver role. I hope you find it a valuable resource for your journey as a caregiver.

Prologue

My Story

Before we get started, I think it's important to share my story and provide a little context for this book.

I'm a nurse, so you think I'd be perfectly prepared to serve as a family caregiver, right? You'd expect that with such great preparation, there would be no road-bumps or potholes in my journey, but there have been many. My husband has Alzheimer's disease. We married late in life, a second marriage for each of us, so we did not expect that either of us would come to the marriage with a clean slate. His mother had the same diagnosis and died with her disease in her eighties. So, the idea that he might fall prey to this disease was certainly on our minds, but in the early years of our relationship, we didn't worry about that as a consequence. We went about our lives and enjoyed the abundance of love we shared.

My husband had always been wary of the familial connection with Alzheimer's and had, for many years throughout mid-life, sought out neuro-psychiatric testing expecting that early-warning signals may show up if he watched for them. None of that testing proved anything. He did not have any signs of early-onset symptoms (disease or diagnosis before age 60). But, in 2010, at the age of 79, he suffered a heart attack, which led to an emergency triple by-pass surgery. Shortly after that procedure, I began to notice little things that confused me. I didn't know that they were the precursors of a fatal, neurologic illness, Alzheimer's disease.

He recovered from open-heart surgery with flying colors – his cardiac surgeon pronounced him "well" and we went on with our lives. But those "little things" were increasingly evident. He had been running a business and was known for a level of orderliness that was the envy of his colleagues. Everything was always filed properly; he could put his hands on any piece of paper without question – he knew where everything was. But soon, uncharacteristic piles started to grow in his office. He had more difficulty gathering materials for a meeting. He would complain that someone had "moved his papers" when in fact he was the only person to venture into his home office, for fear of knocking over an important pile.

By 2012, he had to give up his business because to continue required recertification. By then, he recognized, that he could not study for or expect to pass another certification exam. His brain, which had been his most reliable friend throughout his life, was betraying him. In those early years, even the small deficits made him angry.

He endured the fresh rounds of psycho-social and neurological tests that cataloged his response times, his ability to find words, solve problems, count change and tell time. The first diagnosis he received was Mild Cognitive Impairment, in 2013. This can, and in his case did, progress in short order to Alzheimer's disease. For me, the questions about how quickly his disease progression would move were foremost in my mind. How much longer could he (should he) drive? What help would he need and when? How would this complicate my work-life as an administrative nurse? The questions hit very close to home for me.

It is now 2019 and as I write for all of you, I am writing for myself as well. This journey of family caregiving is not at all the same as what I studied and practiced as a professional nurse. Of course, my training and education were great preparation for the physical care needs he would encounter, but it did not prepare me at all for the personal and emotional pain that accompanies the increasing disability of a husband in my care.

When the person we care for most is in a steady process of loss, whether that loss is physical or cognitive, it is painful to watch, especially when you are powerless to change what is happening. Like most nurses, I am a "card-carrying controller". I like things to function in predictable and well-planned ways. Alzheimer's doesn't accommodate my preferences; it progresses as it will and takes your loved one and the whole family on a journey of erratic and heart-breaking upheaval. Many describe it as a roller coaster. For me, it has been more like a walk in the woods, searching for a path and never being sure what might be around the next bend or behind the big tree ahead.

Alzheimer's disease can change not only the cognitive abilities of its victims but also their personalities and their behavioral responses to every-day circumstances. Some call it the Jekyll and Hyde disease because one moment the one in your care is acting like their usual self, and the next moment they are a total stranger, behaving in ways you have never witnessed before. For some families, these personality swings can be violent. In our house, they have not been that extreme.

So far, my husband has become weepy and sad, seemingly without any precipitating cause. He's become angry and accusatory when he could not understand what was happening around him or the decisions that were being made. He's been angry and sullen when he realizes that his brain is repeatedly betraying him. To date, these events have all been manageable and episodic. Some families experience a much more volatile and dangerous series of events that require the intervention of emergency services or a geriatric neuro-psychologist and even an admission to a psychiatric hospital. We are most fortunate that our journey has not been that distressing.

My husband is now 88 (21 years my senior) and his disease process has changed our lives in many ways. It became the chief circumstance that determined the date of my retirement and even how much or how fully I can engage in any money-earning enterprise. The costs related to his healthcare needs may threaten our financial well-being and even put my own (separate) retirement savings at risk. We've gone through the travails of his need to stop driving (as we were both concerned he would get lost). And, we've given up many of the shared activities that used to fill our leisure time as a result of his increasing cognitive challenges. He can no longer initiate a phone call, use a computer or navigate the neighborhood. Some days he can barely operate the simplest television remote. He can still dress and feed himself but needs reminders to change his clothes or have a meal. He reads the newspaper all day long and each time he picks it up, the day's stories are fresh and new to him. He watches television with little capacity to distinguish the fictional police drama from the day's news stories – they blend and blur together for him now. He rarely knows what day of the week it is without referencing the date on the daily newspaper and cannot recall the current month.

Much of his long-term memory is still pretty solid. He remembers names and family birthdays. He can do the math to figure out his son's age. He knows his birthdate but cannot remember the events of the last birthday he celebrated. If his son takes him out to lunch, he will not remember it by supper time. He participates in a well-crafted adult daycare program that has proven very beneficial to him but, on the days he attends, he has no recollection of the day's events. Each time I get him ready to go to the senior center, he asks me if he's ever been there before and why he needs to go.

Repeated questions, cyclic conversation and the need for endless re-explanation are the issues that drive some Alzheimer's caregivers crazy. That hasn't been too challenging for me, but I am not with him all day, every day, and certainly not his sole, 24/7, caregiver. There are others on our "care team" that shoulder some of the load. As his needs increase, this team will change and grow. I recognize that it is not a job I am able or even willing to do alone. Like so many things in life, *it takes a village*.

Chapter One

Self-care Strategies for Your Physical Needs

Our bodies need a lot of care, even under the best circumstances. This is especially true when we are under unusual stress. Caregiving, even for someone we love, is a stressor and as much as we'd like to dismiss that and say, "I'm fine. I can do this." Often we are not fine and our bodies are feeling the strain of caregiving in ways we may not immediately detect. We are not always tuned in to the clues our bodies send us to let us know that the stress and strain are getting unmanageable and that we need help! Let's look at the physical symptoms.

When we're under stress, we react both emotionally and physically in ways we may not fully understand. A stressful situation – whether something in our physical environment, such as noise from the new airport runway, our work environment, a project deadline or a new supervisor in our interpersonal environment, the changes brought on by an illness in the family, triggers a cascade of responses. Our stress hormones produce a well-orchestrated and physiologically hard-wired set of changes. We may feel our heart begin to pound, our breathing quickens and our muscles may tense. Sweat appears on our forehead and palms, we are anxious, nervous, and on-edge.

This set of reactions to stress is commonly called the fight-or-flight response. Our heart pumps more rapidly, assuring oxygen-rich blood goes to our brain to keep us alert and sharp. Peripheral blood vessels constrict so that most of our blood is directed to our vital organs, which drives up our blood pressure. Adrenalin is pumped into our bloodstream so that we are ready for action. This cascade has been a survival mechanism that has protected us from our earliest times. Prehistoric man encountered life-threatening situations he might not escape. These hormonal changes and physiological responses helped him to fight off the threat or flee to safety. This ancient mechanism for saving us from terrifying threats works fine if the threat is conquered (the saber-tooth tiger is killed) or the threat goes away (the enemy retreats). Unfortunately, in today's world, the threats are more chronic. They are not thwarted; they do not simply go away. As a result, our bodies are confronted with stressor upon stressor and we may remain in a state of overreaction to common, every-day stressors that while not life-threatening, such as traffic jams, work pressure, and family difficulties, are persistent pressures.

In recent years, research has taught us not only how and why these reactions occur but the long-term effects of chronic stress on our physical and psychological health. With repeated activation and re-activation of the stress response, what we call chronic stress, can lead to high blood pressure, promote the formation of artery-clogging deposits (plaque), and cause brain cell changes that can lead to anxiety, depression, and even addiction.

The most current research suggests that our chronic stress may also contribute to obesity and sleep disorders through the persistent release of cortisol, a stress hormone that increases sugars (glucose) in the bloodstream, enhance the brain's use of glucose for energy, and increase the availability of substances that repair tissues, causing sustained inflammation. Cortisol also curtails functions nonessential in a fight-or-flight situation like immune system responses and digestive system activity, reproductive system and natural growth processes. If the immediate threat has passed, but chronic stress sends the message that some lasting threat continues, cortisol may continue to be pumped into the system causing chronic, life-threatening physical problems to our health.

The cure for the stress response is, as Herbert Benson explained years ago in his book, The Relaxation Response (1975). We humans can learn how to counter the stress response by using a combination of approaches that elicit the relaxation response. Given what was available in his day, Benson turned his readers' attention to Transcendental Meditation. Today, there are techniques (which we'll explore at the end of this chapter) available to every one of us. They include Guided Imagery (passive or interactive), Mindfulness Meditation, and Breathing Exercises, all of which can be learned from a practitioner, by using apps on your phone or by exploring the bookstore or Internet. Benson is likely amazed at what he set in motion!

The physical effects of stress are real. All too often, we take the symptoms of our stress to a medical provider who may or may not understand what life has handed us and the amount of stress we may be under. That provider may run a battery of tests and find (or not find) a physical ailment to treat. Then, the treatment may be a medication or a therapy that still does not address the kind or amount of stress the patient is under. It may even dull the symptom, but it doesn't, it can't, solve the problem. That's not to discourage you from discussing symptoms of stress with your medical provider, but be sure to disclose all the information that the provider needs to make a complete and thorough diagnosis. Failing to tell your provider about all the responsibilities that you're managing, orchestrating and taking on for the one in your care can only handicap that provider in giving you wise advice. It is no shame to be stressed. The physical symptoms are real, but you have to treat the CAUSE, not merely the symptoms.

Stress can wreak havoc on your life and your wellbeing. Ignoring it is the fastest path to allowing it to take over your life and dictate your energy levels, your mood, and your wellbeing. Learning to acknowledge it, recognize it and manage it is critical to living a healthy life, in spite of the truth that stressors occur in all our lives, especially when we are family caregivers.

Locate Medical Practitioners who "Get It". This means, if your current provider does not know or understand that you've taken on a caregiving role, they cannot help you in the ways that you may need help. In particular, if the medical provider doesn't know that your level of stress has ramped up over your normal, previous level, that provider can't possibly understand and appreciate how your needs can be addressed. You need and deserve providers (and you may need more than one) who are capable of addressing your needs for medical as well as psychological care.

Build a team around you who can address new needs as they arise. This could include not only a primary care provider, but also a massage therapist, an energy worker, a physical therapist, an exercise trainer, a nutritionist and even a health coach. Each of these services can improve or sustain your physical health in ways that support you through the logical changes that the stress of caregiving brings.

Get some Exercise and Movement. Because we're all different, I want to suggest several kinds of exercise and movement, some of which may appeal to you more than others. Often, it may just be a matter of time. You may not have time for a run, but you do have time for a calming walk to the mailbox; you don't have time to go to the gym, but you do have a few minutes to go up and down the stairs. Having a host of choices available to you, allows you to make whatever level or type of exercise you need accessible in the amount of time you have at the moment. You can always decide to do more movement later when you have more time. Here are some common options:

- **Aerobic exercise** is movement that gets your heart rate elevated to a safe level and challenges your circulatory system. With experience, some people can do aerobic exercise for hours (consider the marathon runner), but most of us have limits to the amount of aerobic work we can do in one session. Experts tell us that to elevate your heart rate for as little as five minutes can create several positive physiologic changes. Many benefits have been ascribed to aerobic exercise, including helping you to:
    o Burn fat and calories if weight loss is your goal.
    o Make your heart strong so that your heart is more effective.

- Increase your lung capacity by causing you to breathe more deeply than usual to feed oxygenated blood to your hard-working muscles.
- Reduce your risk of a heart attack, lower your high cholesterol, help manage your high blood pressure and even help with your diabetes.
- Feel good because, in time, aerobic exercise will permit your brain to release endorphins (think, runner's high) which are the body's feel-good drugs.
- Sleep better without pent-up energy; expending your tension through aerobic exercise can allow muscles to relax once you're done.
- Reduce stress by calming your mind; you're concentrating on your movement, you're watching your route, or you're focused on your breathing and you can let go of whatever is making you stress out.

- **Walking** may or may not be aerobic. It could just be a stroll to the corner, a calm walk around the lake, or an on-foot errand to complete. Whatever it is, walking is a natural physical activity that we learn in our first year (or so) of life and carry with us as a skill and a tool for other meaningful activity. You may just want to get a pedometer or a fitness tracker and see how many steps you take on an average day. This may tell you whether you want to increase that number (for health, fitness or relaxation) or whether you want to decrease that number for joint protection or greater efficiency in your daily routines. Walking can be a way to simply move in a quiet way which you can make mindful with a walking meditation or a repeated mantra, matched to the pace of your gait.
- **Non or Low-Impact Exercise**, a personal trainer may be in a good position to offer you additional suggestions for increasing your activity without risking damage to joints or soft tissues; swimming is a good example. Even if you are not an accomplished swimmer, engaging in a pool aerobics class or just pool play (such as dog-paddling, to keep yourself in

motion) can raise your heart rate and be gentler on your body than workouts on land. If protecting your joints is important for you, finding low-impact exercise is a great option to pursue.

- **Strength training** can be done in the gym with free weights or machines, or done while you watch television with stretch bands, or cans of soup or bottles of water for added weight. By adding just this small amount of additional weight to your movement, repetitious movement suddenly becomes repetitive strength training exercise. You may do this for a set time or merely put your mind to it when the commercials interrupt your favorite TV show. Long patterns or short phases of activity can help you gently stretch and stress a muscle beyond its usual range of movement and increase its capacity to serve you. You don't have to become a bodybuilder to benefit from even a little strength training. This added range of motion can help make any functional activity easier. Functional activities can include climbing the stairs, carrying in the groceries or lifting a child from a car seat. Using our muscle groups in thoughtful, planned, and disciplined ways can make all the daily challenges much easier because our muscles are ready for the work.
- **Stretching** can be as simple as reaching for the stars and then touching your toes to engaging in a complex yoga practice. Your choice about how you stretch and how often you stretch is up to you, but it ought to make you feel good, not achy. Whatever your choice in the arena of stretching, it ought to make you feel refreshed, not exhausted. Watch how often a cat will stretch – and seemingly for the pure joy of the movement.
- **Physical work** that isn't physically intensive may not be something you consider as exercise, but it can be good for you on many levels. Sometimes physical work allows you to simply check off some chore you've needed to accomplish and that is a stress reliever in itself. Other times the repetitive motion of the work may be relaxing – for some, that could be sanding furniture, for others, folding towels. It depends of course, on how you approach the work. But simply being physical to

accomplish a goal can change your focus, burn off some nervous energy and allow you to feel better from the physical work in which you engaged.

Pursue Rest and Sleep as a natural recharger for your body. A body without sleep, especially quality sleep that genuinely allows for rest, rejuvenation and restoration, is a body that will find itself in trouble in short order. Experts tell us we need seven to nine hours of sleep out of every 24-hour day. Better yet, if the sleeping hours are continuous so that our bodies can genuinely rest and relax and feel ready for the coming day. Most of us know that getting a good night's sleep is important, but few adults make solid sleep a priority.

To further complicate our sleep cycle, our typical day may be filled with stimulants like coffee and sugar, caffeinated sodas – both regular and diet, energy drinks, and, irritants like alarm clocks and external lights from electronic devices, which can interfere with our natural sleep/wake cycle. Screen time can take its toll. For many of us simply learning to recognize our patterns may wake us up (pun intended) to the many choices we could make to enhance the sleep we can achieve.

A healthy sleep environment is mostly about where you sleep. Having a bedroom that is quiet, at a cool (rather than hot) temperature, with a mattress you find comfortable and supportive, and dark enough for you to get to sleep relatively quickly is important. While you may not be able to accomplish each of those goals in one sweep of your bedroom, you may be able to control more than you think. *Sleep hygiene* is the term used to describe a host of strategies to build a healthy sleep environment these may include:

- **Invest in a good mattress** is an enormous gift to yourself and others who sleep in your house. A good mattress can lead to less tossing and turning, resulting in more restful sleep and a much better mood in the day to come.
- **Buy black-out blinds** so that the room is adequately dark to promote sleep. This can go a long way toward helping you feel

ready for sleep, feel invited to sleep, and get in sync with your natural circadian rhythms.
- **Decrease needless screen-time** in order to promote the secretion of melatonin. While light of any kind at night can suppress the secretion of melatonin, blue light at night which for most people, predominantly comes from screens and electronic devices can be more powerfully disruptive. Be vigilant about turning off your phone or put it in a drawer; set your bedtime and shut off the television; shut off your computer or don't bring it into bed.
- **Likewise, rise with the sun** by getting up, making the room bright and keeping to a regular schedule whenever possible. It can enhance the likelihood that a pattern of good sleep is in your future.
- **Use comfortable, well-fitting sheets** that stay in place on the mattress and stay tucked in. Not only do sheets need to fit the bed properly, they also need to feel good on your skin. Fabric content and thread count can matter. Avoid sheets that leave you with wrinkles and ridges under your body – these can wake you up and make unnecessary pressure on your skin. To create the best sleep experience you can, you might find it helpful to smooth out the sheets each morning when you make your bed.
- **Sleep alone**, a rare treat for some, and a worthy undertaking for others. This could require some effort, planning, and rearranging of your life (and perhaps the lives of others). However, if sleeping alone is what gets you to a good night's sleep, no one, especially not someone who loves you, should stand (or lie) in your way and that includes your four-legged sleeping partners, Fido and Spot.
- **A regular pattern for waking and sleeping** builds a rhythm that meets your sleep needs. It requires that you go to bed at the same time each evening and rise at the same time each morning. You can adjust those times if your days and nights are switched, perhaps due to shift work or to attend to the care needs of your

one in your cares. Set an intention for a solid night's sleep. Turn off all electrical distractions such as your TV, phone, and laptop.
- **Night-time rituals** are helpful in signaling to your overactive mind that it is time to go to sleep. Some examples include:
    - **Ablutions** – often thought of as a ceremonial act of washing parts of the body – this can mean brushing your teeth, washing your face, removing make-up or jewelry you don't want to wear to bed.
    - **Clearing off the day** – means to take off your day-clothes and put on night-clothes.
    - **Preparing your bed** – by pulling back the sheets and bedding, adding a scent to your bed linens (lavender can be soothing), and adding or removing layers of covers to keep your bed at the right temperature for your best sleep.
    - **Developing a sleep-inducing pattern** – could be enhanced by a CD created for relaxation that puts you to sleep. It could be music you love and find soothing. It could be repeating a meditative mantra or rehearsing your gratitude list for the day. Each of us develops one or more routines that help us slide toward sleep, explore what might work best for you and employ it every night.
    - **Setting the stage for a good night's sleep** includes setting aside our worries of the day. If we go to bed with worries, they stay with us all night. So, what are you worried about? Are there chores you've left undone that will poke at your brain all night if you don't get them done? Whatever is troubling you, find a way to set it aside for the night:
        - Write down chores you worry you might forget, so they are safely on *the list* for tomorrow and don't need to trouble you all night.
        - Keep a notebook by the bed, and when thoughts wake you up, jot them down so you can deal with them when your head is clearer.
        - Have a back-to-sleep strategy to use if you find your sleep interrupted. This could be the same CD you used

- Making up for lost time when your life demands it is easily done through a "cat nap". Napping is a strategy we've all employed at some time in our lives. It may have been the between-class-siestas we enjoyed in college or the between-feedings-snooze we needed when raising our babies; naps can be a natural part of anyone's experience. The National Sleep Foundation reminds us that "while naps do not necessarily make up for inadequate or poor-quality nighttime sleep, a short nap of 20-30 minutes can help to improve mood, alertness and performance" (https://sleepfoundation.org/sleep-topics/napping). That's a good thing if you're being robbed of regular, restful sleep. Just don't think it can be an enduring substitute.

to get to sleep originally, it could be that mantra that worked for you earlier or continuing the gratitude list that reminds you that there is much to be thankful for.

Invite Relaxation is a gift you can give to yourself regardless of what's driving your stress. I'll offer you more details on what may be causing you stress in the chapters on Emotional Strategies and Spiritual Strategies, but for now, consider both what would allow you to relax and how you might deliberately allow yourself to relax.

What would allow you to relax is very personal choice. It may be cutting your 'to do' list by a few hundred items. For me, this means accepting that things are good enough, even when I know that in most circumstances I'd like it all to be perfect. As long as I'm a family caregiver, I need to lighten my load and take myself off the hook for being perfect. In my case, I manage my chores by asking:

- Is my house clean enough (so that no one will become ill from staying there)?
- Are our meals healthy enough (perhaps not gourmet, but to keep us alive and well)?

- Are our clothes comfortable and clean (rather than stylish and fashion-forward)?
- Is my time distributed fairly enough (to give everyone who wants some of my time at least a bit of what I have to offer)?

Sometimes, the redistribution of my priorities is important – especially at the holidays, when priorities may shift. On the weekends, activities may need to be adjusted. I need to acknowledge how much time, energy and effort caregiving requires and be kind and compassionate to myself as I make the ever-changing adjustments to my priorities. I also need to make sure that I'm addressing my own priorities, and not just struggling to satisfy everyone else's demands and expectations.

The answer to how to relax can be found in the resources available to you. This may require calling on other people who have depended on you for ages, to manage their own lives and to do more for the family cause. We're constantly reminded that raising a child requires a village. It also takes a village to care for the needs of the one in your care who has become highly dependent on you. For me, there is little or no family who can come to the rescue, so early-on I worked hard to build a team of friends and colleagues who would, if called, contribute whatever they could at the time. That team currently has about 10 members. Not all of them are free to come when I call, but each of them responds as able when the need arises. They have helped me move furniture, remove clutter and they've even cooked me meals when that was the need at hand. My team/village is an invaluable and necessary resource!

Others find that calling in outside help can afford them a few hours of freedom when they need it most. What you do with that free time is entirely up to you. Get some pampering at the spa, get your hair cut, go shopping and enjoy some retail therapy, eat out, have a treat, go to a movie, meet with a friend, visit the library, play nine holes of golf, wash the car, find a pick-up game of basketball, read a book, take on a walking path around a park, explore nature – do something that brings you joy! Above all, do not give in to feelings of guilt that you are not doing your job. You deserve and, more importantly, you need a break.

Every one of us who is caring for another can fall prey to the physical symptoms of the stress that comes with the added load of caregiving. Making sure we take care of our own physical needs throughout that time of caregiving is essential for the wellbeing of ourselves and for the person(s) we care for. It follows the principle reiterated to us each time we fly on an airplane, *"Please put your own oxygen mask on before assisting others!"*

Ideas for How to Relax. Here are some tools which may allow you to invite rest and relaxation when you are stressed or distracted by the cares of life:

- **Guided Imagery** – Many recordings exist online and on CD to assist you in finding a relaxed state through the use of imagery. Imagery is simply the way we create mental pictures that enrich our thought patterns. Unfortunately, we use imagery when we worry, which is what can make our worries so vivid. But, you can recruit the same capacity for relaxation by allowing a script (one you purchase or one you record yourself) you calmly listen to, take you to a calm and restful place in your imagination. Such a quiet journey may only take a few minutes but can bring prolonged positive effects including inducing sleep.
- **Deep Breathing Techniques** – There are many varieties of breathing exercises you can employ to relax your mind and body. One is simply belly-breathing; allowing your in-breath to lift your belly and, on the out-breath, allowing your belly to slowly sink. Attention to this rhythm can be enhanced by putting your hand on your belly as your breath enables it to rise and then fall.

    Another breathing exercise is called square-breathing which is simply managing and holding your breath for a specific count to slow down the rate and rhythm. We think of this breathing pattern as square because it has four parts, for example: Breathe in for the count of 4; Hold your breath for the count of 4; Breathe out to the count of 4; Hold your breath for the count

of 4. Then repeat the sequence, extending the count to suit your preferences.
- **Music Therapy** – While there is an entire professional field for music therapists, using music for your own relaxation does not require a professional. You can select any music that relaxes or calms you or, you can select sounds of nature (such recordings are readily available commercially) that you find comforting and use them as your soundtrack. Often when you have selected a perfect playlist for your rest and relaxation, you may find that you fall asleep listening to this comforting sound. Headphones or earbuds can enhance the effect.
- **Progressive Relaxation** – While it may be easiest to learn this technique by listening to a recorded script or having the benefit of a reader who will speak the instructions to you, once practiced, it is fairly easy to repeat on your own and without prompting. Progressive relaxation is the conscious tightening and relaxing of muscle groups in a sequence (usually from feet to head) that follows the body. It is best practiced lying down, supine (on your back), and with at least fifteen minutes to devote to the experience.

  Begin by breathing deeply to signal your body to change its focus and then tighten a group of muscles to their limit. When that limit is reached, you release those tightened muscles and permit them to fully relax – a good place to start is with your toes on both feet. After the toes have fully relaxed, move your attention to the arches of your feet and repeat the process. Proceed up your legs, with calves, thighs, buttocks, etc., and repeat for your fingers, arms and shoulders. Most people who practice progressive relaxation end with tightening and relaxing the neck and finally facial muscles, which can noticeably relieve headache symptoms for some people.

Chapter Two

Self-care Strategies for your Emotional Needs

What is an emotional need? How do you define it and sort emotional needs out from all the other human needs? An emotional need emerges from basic feelings like love, fear, anger, sorrow, anxiety, frustration, and sadness. It involves and includes the need for understanding, empathy, and support of another person. Often when we are caregivers, especially if we are a caregiver for a spouse, we may have lost the familiar, primary relationship through which many of our emotional needs have long been fulfilled. A spouse dealing with a physical illness or injury may not have the capacity to be there for you as they were in the past. And certainly, a spouse with dementia or a traumatic brain injury may not be able to recover the former supportive behaviors that you've come to enjoy as a partner. That is a very hard loss to sustain.

We all have emotional needs. Sometimes we expect them and they are socially understood – we weep at weddings or christenings because our heart is full of love and empathy for the people in the ceremony. We shriek on the rollercoaster because the gravity-defying plunge terrifies us (in a good way). We cry at the movies when the guy wins the girl or the Titanic sinks or the happily-ever-after ending comes. We laugh at the comedian, the cat videos on YouTube and the funny story told by a friend. But, emotional needs and feelings can also bubble to the surface when we least expect them, and at times, they aren't socially understood or accepted.

Sometimes we hit emotional road bumps or potholes. They seemingly come out of nowhere and make us cry or swear or throw a plate; signs of personal eruption sneak up on us and catch us (and others) by surprise. Some people deal better with these surprises than others. Figuring out how you deal with them is worthwhile. Paying attention to your reaction when an emotional pothole catches you by surprise will enable you to figure out what emotional needs lie just beneath the surface of your well-kept façade. We are well-trained to smile in spite of our circumstances (especially health care professionals). That can be good advice, sometimes. But when it adds to your load of *shoulds, oughts* and *musts* – then it becomes unhealthy.

I'm reminded of a classic song performed by Smokey Robinson and the Miracles, called *Tears of a Clown*. The opening lines from that song say, "Now if there's a smile on my face, it's only there trying to fool the public. But when it comes down to fooling you, now honey that's quite a different subject" (Crosby, Robinson & Wonder, 1967). A lot of us go through life like that, putting on a happy face, thinking everyone is fooled by our sweet demeanor. But the realities of caregiving often lead to a deep, emotional well-spring of feelings, emotions, needs and deficits. We can hide them for a while, but people who know us and care about us will notice that something isn't right.

The difficulty comes, not from the feelings we experience or the needs we have, but from our misguided assumption that those who love and care about us can read our minds. Since no one can read our minds, that means, that if we ever expect our emotional needs to be met, we have to share them with others. We have to say what is on our hearts and minds, even (and especially) when it hurts. We only injure and disappoint ourselves when we expect that others can see precisely what we're feeling and respond from that special knowledge. They don't know if you don't tell them. Finding some safe, caring people and places where you can share your heart is critically important to your emotional health.

People also say things that can unintentionally add to the hurt you may be shouldering. They say meaningless and thoughtless things that are either platitudes or well-intentioned nonsense. You can't stop them from saying what they believe to be true (which is mostly about helping them cope with their own discomfort), but you can prepare yourself for the pain they may inflict by protecting yourself from taking them too seriously.

I've heard thoughtless people say to a non-believer, "It's in God's hands!" or after a death, say of the one in your care, "He's in a better place." And even relatives, who you think would understand, have been heard saying, "He seems fine to me!" If only they would walk a mile in your shoes, they might understand what is really going on and appreciate the level of wear and tear your care recipient's condition places on you.

For your own mental health and the sake of all your relationships, don't expect others to change – they probably won't. However, you have choices. You can accept the callous comments and let them beat you down or you can let them fall off you like rain and be grateful for all the well-wishing people in your life, even when they say things that startle or offend you. If you have one or two confidantes in your life, be sure to let them know how much you appreciate their ability to hear and respond to you from a loving heart. Those kinds of friends are gold, and to be treasured. Just remember, people do their best to find the appropriate thing to say based on their own experiences and discomfort. More than likely they mean well, it just isn't communicated that well.

Emotional needs are real, they deserve to be acknowledged. And, whenever possible, they need to be addressed and met. It may not be possible to fill every need you find in yourself, but if you deny that you have any emotional needs, you are likely on a path to self-destruction. These needs are genuine, they are human and they are worth tending to with care. Sometimes this gentle chore will be done by others, but more often than not, we must learn to tend to our own emotional needs – largely because you are the only the person to know what it would take to fill that need. So as you identify a need, take time to ask yourself, what would meet that need, what would address the deficit?

Sometimes the answer may be a good cry; other times it may be a good laugh. These are acts of self-care and cannot be given to you by anyone else – no matter how close or how long your relationship. It is often the simplest response that can give you what you need. Let that answer come from within.

> My experience: *For me, crying in the shower was my go-to coping mechanism especially in the early years of caregiving. My husband wouldn't hear me and my face wouldn't look streaked with tears if I was wet all over from the shower. Later, I admitted that I needed to see a therapist and found a psychologist who understood my situation. Discussions with her helped me recognize that I was depressed, so adding an antidepressant medication also became part of my self-care regimen. Still later, when I had built stronger, more sufficient coping mechanisms for myself, the medication was no longer necessary. The first step was simply admitting that it hurt. Then, the second step was seeking the help needed to manage the pain.*

It may also be advantageous to meet (deliberately) with a professional or peer helper. A counselor or therapist, life coach, trusted clergy-person, a social worker, psychologist or medical provider may be someone you can see and talk about your emotional needs. There is no shame in that. We all have needs, but we don't all have a personal relationship that can address our needs – so, it is important to find such a supportive person.

Support groups, especially those geared toward the specific caregiving need that fills your life, such as caring for a spouse with cancer or a parent with dementia, can be very beneficial – in person or even online. Sharing with others who understand what you are dealing with every day, because they deal with the same or similar circumstances, can bring amazing relief. Conversations with others who are also in caregiving roles can normalize your own situation. You begin to realize that you are not the only one faced with sadness, frustration or loss. Finding and building a support system, in whatever form you can, is a necessary and worthwhile endeavor.

This access to a caring community can keep you from feeling all alone with your emotional needs and only feeling worse with your own company. Generally, we caregivers call that a "pity party" which, can serve us well for a few moments. However, if you indulge self-pity for very long, you can make yourself miserable! There is nothing wrong with acknowledging that your life as a caregiver is difficult, that you are lonely or that you are exhausted. But to simply sit in that sadness and not take action to deal with those feelings is not in your best interest.

You may have to try several avenues before you land on those individuals or groups that match your needs, your style and your preferences. As you encounter a new opportunity to share yourself, give yourself that time to "try it on for size" so you can make sure that place or group or person makes you feel comfortable and well-supported. You don't have to bear your soul with everyone you meet. However, you can share what feels safe at first and, as relationships build, share more of yourself in time. But learning that you can open up, you can let others see what's troubling you, is a very enriching and rewarding experience.

Once you can acknowledge that you do have emotional needs, you can begin to sort them out – on your own or with help from a friend or professional. You have likely seen Maslow's Hierarchy of Needs. Maslow, an acclaimed psychologist wrote in his 1943 paper "A Theory of Human Motivation" in Psychological Review, that we all have basic needs and until one level of need (the most basic needs) is filled, it is impossible to address those of a higher level (Maslow, 1943). Later, authors expounded on his work using a visual aid in the form of a pyramid.

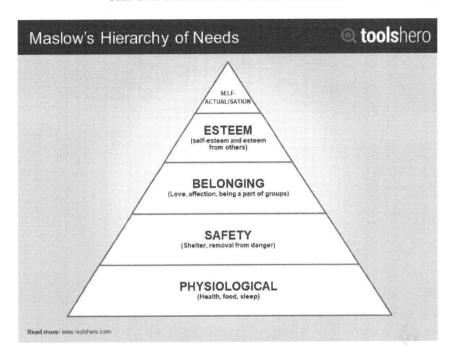

On the base of the pyramid are the first and most basic needs. He saw these as Physiological Needs. Think of these as the need for food, water, warmth, rest and exercise, and hygiene. Recognizing these as basic needs as essential for life itself, makes us realize that people struggling to put food on the table, would logically feel stress and anxiety. But, when you're caring for a family member who is dependent on you for basic care, you are dealing at the level of these basics. If it is a challenge to feed the one in your care, to keep them clean, you bear the burden of managing these very basic and essential needs.

The second level Maslow labeled as Safety Needs. Some of us might think of our finances as part of that sense of safety, so, when caregiving challenges our capacity to pay bills, earn money or keep a job we love, our safety needs are threatened.

Other safety needs could be what we think of as the "social safety net" in the United States. For many caregivers, that means the capacity to tap into Medicaid or Medicare to live safely and with access to the healthcare system. If your health insurance needs are fully addressed, you may not feel that you have safety needs. But since many caregivers are one paycheck away from financial calamity – often because of the enormous costs of the disability or circumstances of one in their care – you can appreciate that stress and anxiety may be present for many families on this level.

Moving up the hierarchy, Maslow labeled the third level as Love and Belonging Needs. While the first two levels can drive emotional needs and feelings, this level is all about emotional needs. Brené Brown, a social researcher, and professor at the University of Houston, in her Ted Talk on Shame and Vulnerability recorded in June 2010, says, "We are hardwired to connect with others, it's what gives purpose and meaning to our lives, and without it there is suffering."

We really cannot avoid the need for love and belonging, the need for connection – is in our physiology, in our psychology – it is an intrinsic part of who we are as humans. If, as a caregiver, you cannot connect to the one in your care as you once did due to a physical or neurological disability, you may suffer from that loss of connection. Others may not understand it, but for many of us, who care for someone with dementia, the personality of that individual changes over time and the person they were – the person we knew seems gone from us. That person with dementia may forget your name, not recognize your face; that disease-driven loss of intimate knowing is exactly what Maslow understood as a common human need.

Maslow's fourth level he called Esteem Needs – these are the feelings we have about ourselves (self-esteem) and the impressions we make on others which they reflect back to us (other-esteem). When you think of yourself as an artistic painter, you need to paint, to create art. When you think of yourself as a wife, you need to define yourself in relation to the life and home you've created with your spouse. When you think of yourself as a teacher, you need a mind that supports you in thinking and instructing others. Age, illness and disability can rip from our lives the acts and opportunities that have given our lives meaning. Our Esteem Needs demonstrate that when we feel a loss of meaning in our lives those feelings are real and when they cannot be fulfilled, we grieve them and we seem lost without them. Caregiving can be a thankless role, especially in comparison to other roles we've enjoyed in life that bring us appreciation and praise; contributing to a loss of self-esteem.

For a caregiver, who has to cut back on working hours or left a job entirely in order to fulfill the caregiver role, there can be a real loss both in terms of valuable income and a sense of being a valued employee. For the spouse who found fulfillment in community engagement or social gatherings, the isolation of the caregiver role may add to the sense of loss and a fear of missing out on happier days.

This sense of loss can also be true for the recipient of care as much as for the caregiver. None of us prepares in advance to be in need of care from others, so it goes to reason that the golfer who has suffered a stroke and cannot golf may be miserable. The artist who can no longer create art may be frustrated.

In my household, it is the businessman who can no longer make sound decisions and is reminded daily of his disability who is often distressed beyond words. As caregivers, we may be feeling those needs or watching those needs. We may find ourselves unable to be fulfilled as we once were or to help the one who requires care find fulfillment. Caregiver and care recipient may each feel this frustration.

We may find we've given up our pleasures and self-fulfilling activities because it is difficult to pursue them and be a caregiver, too. We stop seeing friends because they do not know what to say to us. We stop going out because the now unfamiliar or rule-bound environment of the restaurant or theater is too challenging for the one in our care to enjoy. This can leave the caregiver feeling lonely, lost, disconnected and even disregarded. It is as if because we care for someone in need, we have become invisible. This can be evidence that esteem needs are not being met. What is worse is that we may begin to think of ourselves in lesser terms, "I'm only a caregiver." You are not. You are a complex human being with many capabilities and longings. Do not give up on yourself and do not lose yourself into the caregiver role. Which, I acknowledge, is easier said than done.

Finally, at the very top layer of Maslow's pyramid is Self-Actualization. Self-Actualization cannot be achieved unless all the other levels of need have been fully addressed.

Caregiving is rarely self-actualizing; it can be but don't expect it to be. I have heard caregivers speak with tenderness and awe about moments that moved them, stirred them to their soul when they experienced that rare sense of privilege as a caregiver. It may come at the moment your care recipient says, "thank you!" It may come after a restless day when your care recipient finds sleep. It may come in some small, unexpected success that appears in a flash and then is gone. These are moments every caregiver must learn to cherish because they are rare and fleeting.

Additionally, I want to acknowledge that there are caregivers who are looking after the needs of a family member who caused them pain earlier in life – like the abusive or neglectful parent, who is now in need of their service and care. This can add a layer of incredible difficulty to the caregiving situation and may require additional supports just to accomplish the work of caregiving. If this is your circumstance, it is important not to dismiss the real traumas of the past and to seek out help that may bring you, some healing of that past.

For anyone who serves in this role around the clock, 24/7, tender moments can be fleeting and difficult to find. Feelings of self-actualization are often very elusive while you are in a caregiver role. The important thing is to be able to separate all the other parts of your self-identity from that role you fill as a caregiver. You are more than your role. You are more than the survivor in the present conditions in which you labor. Remember that you are more than the doer of chores, the cook, housekeeper, nurse-maid, laundry washer and folder, bed-maker, etc. that the caregiver role demands of you.

At every one of Maslow's levels, we have emotional needs. Acknowledging them, attending to them, addressing them in a variety of ways will enable us to survive the painful reminder that all is not "well" within our household. There may be illness, pain, loss, and disability, but there can also be safety, security, love and connectedness -- embrace that possibility. And, take heart in the realization that you are more than the chores you must do.

To summarize:

- Emotional needs emerge from basic human feelings.

- Serving as a caregiver will bring up many emotional needs – for you, and for the recipient of your care.
- Everyone has emotional needs, but situations that make us feel out-of-control (caregiving is one) can bring them to the surface more easily.
- Covering up our emotional needs is a coping mechanism that may not serve you well as a caregiver – you need someone you can confide in.
- People will say thoughtless things as if they understand what you are going through. Usually, they don't know that they have hurt your feelings. Don't take their comments too seriously.
- We cannot change other people. We can only change our own personal responses to them.
- Acknowledging and tending to your own emotional needs is essential self-care skill.
- Ignoring or denying your own emotional needs will only make your emotional upheaval worse.
- Seeking peer support or help from a professional can be an excellent way to get through emotional pain.
- We all experience the occasional pity-party but learning to move on and do something to genuinely help the situation is an important skill to build. Don't wallow too long in your own self-pity.
- Seek out a caring community.
- Human needs follow Maslow's Hierarchy of Needs – think through where you are and where your needs are the greatest at any given time. Recognize how important it is to address them.
- Don't give up on your own self-actualization. For many of us, there is life after caregiving and once our circumstances are different we must be prepared to get back into the activities of life that bring us joy.

How to Find Resources for your Emotional Needs –

We live in an amazing age when resources can be right at our fingertips even if they do not exist at all in the community where we live. The Internet and even specific apps designed just for your specific needs may have exactly what you're looking for. I do not want to presume that I am an Internet wizard or know exactly where to send you but I would urge you to ask the professional clinicians around you where such resources can be located.

Consider too, that disease and condition-based websites (Alzheimer's Association, American Cancer Society, Diabetes Association, etc.) all have web-based tools and resources you can turn to depending upon your specific needs. Additionally, the AARP (formerly the American Association of Retired Persons) has taken a significant interest in caregivers in our society and have posted a number of valuable resources specifically for caregivers on their website.

In your community, look to see what agencies and organizations may have resources and subject matter experts available to you. Some may offer support groups or access to a social worker or case manager. Others may provide social events that get you out of the house and accommodate the needs of your care recipient as well. One agency may lead you to where daycare, respite care, counseling and other services can be made available.

You may have to do the search but, the tools at your disposal; phone, Internet, word of mouth, can and often do, lead you to the resources you need as a family caregiver.

Chapter Three

Self-care Strategies for your Educational Needs

Maya Angelou once said, "I did then what I knew how to do. Now that I know better, I do better." That is true for all of us. But in order to know better, we have to learn. That learning may begin in the doctor's office or the hospital when a diagnosis is received that has serious consequences for the future, but it does not end there. Collins and Swartz, physicians examining the data available at the time, reported that the "majority of caregivers (81 percent) feel inadequately trained for the skills that they perform, having never received any formal education in caregiving" (Collins & Swartz, 2011).

Feinberg, Reinhard, Houser, and Choula, representing the AARP Public Policy Institute in a 2011 publication, *The Growing Contributions and Costs of Family Caregiving*, cited a 2002 study by Donelan and several colleagues, that made these important assessments about the state of the caregiver burden related to the physical chores of caregiving:

- "Three out of four family caregivers who provided medical/nursing tasks were managing medications, including administering intravenous fluids and injections.

- Almost half were administering 5 to 9 prescription medications a day; one in five was helping with ten or more prescription medications a day.
- Most of these family caregivers learned how to manage at least some of the medications on their own. Many found this work difficult because it was time-consuming and inconvenient, they were afraid of making a mistake, and/or the care recipient would not cooperate.
- More than a third (35%) of family caregivers who provided medical/nursing tasks reported doing wound care.
- While fewer caregivers performed wound care tasks than medication management, a greater percentage of them (66%) identified it as difficult and many (38%) would like more training. Of these caregivers, close to half (47%) were afraid of making a mistake and/or harming their family member" (Feinberg, Reinhard, Houser & Choula, 2011).

Figuring out how to educate yourself on the crucial components of the disease or condition affecting the one in your care is essential to not only that person's wellbeing and safety, but to your own. This education comes from a wide array of sources and since we humans do not all share a single learning style, we must pursue the information we need from the sources available and that resonate with us as adult learners. *No one size fits all!*

There are several ways to begin your educational journey. If your service in the role of family caregiver goes on for an extended time, you will surely acquire a doctoral degree in understanding the disease process or illness the one in your care is facing. More importantly, you will learn to tailor what you learn to the specific needs as they present themselves in your household because, while there are similarities, no two patients/persons are exactly the same. The pattern of your loved one's illness may not follow the exact trajectory you read about in books or hear about from others facing the same diagnosis. Humans respond as individuals and you must figure out how to apply what you learn to the circumstances in which you enact your caregiver role.

There are many junctures at which you will be called upon to make challenging decisions either with or for the person who is ill and requires care. Being educated and well-prepared for these encounters will enable you to make those decisions thoughtfully and without regret. There are many people, authors, professionals and friends who will be your teachers. The person you are caring for will likely be one of those teachers, and probably the most important one. It will be your job to weigh each set of circumstances and, from the standpoint of informed consent, determine what must be done on each occasion. It is not an easy role but being well prepared with a clear understanding of what is known about the disease or condition and its common path of progression will enable you to anticipate at least some of the many difficult decisions you will face.

- **Understanding the Diagnosis** – It is tempting to simply Google a medical diagnosis and assume that the information you will find online is sufficient and adequately accurate for your needs. Those are risky assumptions. Websites are not all created equal and in seeking information of a medical nature, you need to look for sites that are curated and managed by reputable organizations.
- **Start with your own Providers** – Ask your clinicians for detailed information about diagnoses. Also, ask about websites you can safely use for information about drug recommendations, treatment options, research outcomes and evidence related to the care you may be encountering. Read the literature you are given, although there may be more than you can digest in a single reading – keep it available and look through it as you have time and energy to do so. Bookmark the website locations you find most valuable so they are at your fingertips and you don't have to repeatedly search for them. Information changes as the science of healthcare advances and what was true five years ago may not be up to date for today's decision making. That is another reason why you must rely on reputable websites where

the information is updated regularly and where the knowledge behind the information you find is constantly kept current.

A diagnosis is a curious thing. Sometimes it is a relief to get a name for the symptoms your care recipient has been exhibiting; sometimes it is discouraging, because the diagnosis itself may carry a set of expectations about the course of the illness or condition and its probable outcomes. Either way, once you know the diagnosis, you may want and need to learn about it and seek out reliable sources for the specific diagnosis. The Agency for Healthcare Research and Quality (AHRQ), (https://www.ahrq.gov), a website clinicians trust, offers a good booklet outlining the next steps to take, once a diagnosis is determined. Their publication, *"Next Steps after your Diagnosis: Finding Information and Support"*, can be found at:

https://www.ahrq.gov/sites/default/files/publications2/files/diaginfo.pdf

There is another curious truth about diagnoses; sometimes they change. An illness that looks like one thing in its early occurrence may, over time, turn out to be something else. This can be very disrupting to think you know what is going on, only to learn that perhaps the first diagnosis was not the final diagnosis. This can be disconcerting for your healthcare providers as well. Once they've set their expectations in a given direction, it may be difficult for them to let go of that and move in an entirely different direction. But, remember, medicine is pursued as a science, which is ever-changing, revealing new truths to those who study it. What we knew decades ago may be quickly archaic in the light of new discoveries in the scientific world. Be patient with your clinicians who may be just as surprised as you to learn the diagnosis is not as straightforward as first assumed.

- **What to Expect with a Diagnosis; Learning about the Usual Trajectory (prognosis)** – Everyone seems to expect that with a diagnosis comes a crystal ball that can predict how things will go. How long does he have? What can I expect will happen next? What will be the signs that she's getting worse? What will tell us whether the treatment is working? A diagnosis leads us to a hundred new questions, yet many of them are without a definitive answer. Remember, every patient is different, a unique individual with his or her own responses to illness. The path for one person is not necessarily a road-map for the next person, but we can learn from the scientific literature what patterns the disease, illness or condition are likely to reveal.

While the diagnosis may leave you in shock, you may need to be prepared to get up to speed very quickly. Start a notebook (consider a 3-ring notebook) where you can record your questions and the responses from the clinicians; and, make it easy to refer back to the information in one easy-to-find repository. Do not hesitate to ask the medical providers, "Are there things I am forgetting to ask you?" And, do not apologize if you need them to repeat information already stated. If you can, take a trusted friend with you to the appointment who can step in on your behalf with additional questions if you become overwhelmed.

Learn the hallmarks of what to expect. Ask questions and listen carefully to the answers. Your healthcare provider team may not know exactly what will happen next. This is especially true when a new treatment is in use or when the one in your care participates in a clinical trial which is, in itself, an experiment to learn about the potential outcomes from a treatment. It is hard to be patient when it is the very life of the one in your care that is impacted by the course of action, but often science does not know or has not learned exactly what to tell you to expect.

Knowing the prognosis does not mean you resign yourself to the inevitable. It means understanding the likely time-frame in which you must take action and prepare yourself for the course ahead. If there is (as in many cancer treatments) a course of treatment that requires several rounds of chemotherapy, it is prudent to prepare for the long and often arduous emotional and physical trek this journey will require. Knowing the prognosis helps you get yourself ready to support the work ahead, whether that is for a few weeks, a few months or even for years to come.

Also knowing the prognosis helps you and the one in your care make decisions. This is especially true in dementia. Making arrangements for dealing with the myriad issues related to healthcare, financial decisions, and quality of life, especially with someone whose memory is compromised requires that they be able to participate in these arrangements when they are in their best state of mind. This means that some things must be done early, as soon as a diagnosis is received. Wills, advance directives, naming of healthcare proxies, determining durable power of attorney, etc. are not preparations that you can put off. It may be difficult to face the reality that such end-of-life planning must be done now, but to delay means that the person with dementia, for example, will have less and less opportunity to have a say in declaring the priorities that matter most to him or her. Knowing the prognosis may light a fire under you or put more items on your 'to-do' list immediately after the diagnosis and get you and the one in your care moving on tasks for which you may have been procrastinating. But, getting them done will afford you (both) a serious measure of relief when those decisions have been made and put in order.

- **Preparing for the future: legally, financially and with sound end-of-life decisions** – Money is a messy matter for many people. We live in a culture that has long avoided discussions about money – even between people in a marriage or committed relationship. Younger generations, I am learning, are far more willing to openly talk about the financial realities of their lives. But, if you are among the more reticent, you may need to bolster your courage and have these discussions anyway.

Earlier I named some of the end-of-life decisions we all should accomplish, and more definitive lists can be found on a variety of websites. I frequently rely on the Alzheimer's Association's brochure, *End-of-Life Decisions: Honoring the Wishes of a Person with Alzheimer's Disease*. It is available at: https://www.alz.org/national/documents/brochure_endoflifedecisions.pdf

The first step is often the most difficult. And, that is certainly true in beginning the conversation about end-of-life arrangements. But, asking your loved one what he or she wants in terms of quality of life is a critical conversation you must find the courage to have.

Examining and exploring your values (which may be the same or different from the patient's values) about treatment choices; recognizing what matters most as a disease forces difficult choices; getting clear on the realities of how to pay for care and treatment, are all essential parts of this conversation. Each of these topics is a challenging discussion in itself, but altogether they are pretty overwhelming. And, it is critical to you to conquer them before it becomes a painful reality you've never discussed.

Assistance in such conversations may be available from your clinical team. Among the most helpful members of that team will be the social worker who is trained to look at all these aspects of illness and the social and familial consequences a health crisis can create. A social worker may not have all the answers you need but can steer you in the direction of other informational and financial supports that you can explore over time. The key is to avoid delay. The earlier you begin to have these conversations, the more opportunity you will have to reach thoughtful conclusions and make meaningful decisions. Planning is one of the most important gifts you can give to those you love.

- **Recognizing condition changes that need to be addressed** – When you spot changes that need to be made, don't assume you need to tackle them alone. Whether it involves changes to your routines or changes to the space where you live – having a team to help you through those alterations is an enormous benefit. The team may change depending upon the needs of the moment but, never be afraid to ask for what you need. Not everyone can help you move furniture or bring casseroles to stash in the freezer, but each of your team members, friends, family, neighbors, even new acquaintances, has time and talents to share especially if they know what it is you need.

- **Making decisions about health interventions** – Earlier I mentioned advance directives and naming of healthcare proxies. The language for all this may be different in your state or country, so talk to experts in the field (social workers, healthcare providers, your attorney, etc.) to learn what is required where you live. An advance directive will help others (family, healthcare providers, your support team) know what you and the one in your care have chosen about care decisions. It is worth considering that both you, and the one in your care, should have such documents completed, each with your own answers. Common questions within these documents will include:
    o Do you want Cardio-Pulmonary Resuscitation (CPR) if your heart should stop?
    o Do you want intravenous hydration (an IV) if you're not able to drink water?
    o Do you want antibiotics (Oral? By injection? By IV?) if you have an infection?
    o Do you want to be intubated (have a breathing tube and a ventilator) if you cannot breathe on your own?
    o Do you want a feeding tube if you are not able to eat or swallow on your own?

    These questions are important because the answers can determine the focus of attention when your health (or one in your care's health) reaches the end-of-life stage where decisions must be made. Having the answers well thought out ahead of time, documented and shared with key people in your life, can make all the difference in the quality of life when the end of life is nearing. You can Google the phrase "advance care directive online form" and get access to generic forms from organizations you will recognize or find your state's form. Sometimes there is a modest charge for such forms, but it is worth it to have your wishes documented.

Many states have adopted a tool that goes beyond the advance directive – it is a medical order for end-of-life care (in Minnesota, it is called POLST: Provider Orders for Life Sustaining Treatment). The benefit of such a document is that in real life, the people who take care of us in emergencies are first responders, paramedics and emergency medical technicians – they do not make medical decisions, they depend on licensed providers to do that. By securing a medical order for end-of-life care, they have "orders" available to help steer their actions. The most common place to keep such a document is on your refrigerator – most first responders are trained to look there.

It can also be wise to keep copies of these essential documents in a variety of handy places. Many caregivers keep their documents (like advance directives, POLST, durable power of attorney, etc.) on a flash-drive or tablet, with paper copies filed in the house, in the car, at the cabin, and send an extra copy to family members or trusted neighbors so that they will never be without the documentation they may need.

- **Acknowledging the time for palliative care** – Palliative care is the term used to acknowledge that our attention will focus on the patient's comfort taking priority over cure. Sometimes palliative care is called for because all medical interventions have been tried, and there are no more treatment options available. Sometimes, however, it is a choice because the person who is ill does not want to endure one more round of chemotherapy, or one more surgery, or one more radiation treatment. This is a choice that should be honored.

  Recently, Barbara Bush, wife of former U.S. President George H.W. Bush, suffering from congestive heart failure and chronic obstructive pulmonary disease, offered a public statement saying she had decided, "not to seek additional medical treatment and will focus on comfort care" (Bailey & Aleccia, 2018). She died later that year. Her bravery in making her choice about palliative care public helped millions consider that this is indeed a choice, and something each of us should think about.

All too often we equate palliative care with hospice – they are not the same. Hospice is a service that is available in many places to persons who are not expected to live beyond six months (generally). It is a service that is commonly called in far too late in the process. Bringing in hospice earlier can be beneficial to both the person who is ill and the family members caring for him or her. Palliative care may include hospice care or, it may be a decision made for its own benefit.

- **Responding to the endless "side issues" that occur.** Side issues can be almost anything. Some of the issues that require attention, and that we have experienced in our household include:
  o **What new routines must we adopt?** The need to keep a calendar, whether to track medications or medical appointments may become a new requirement for you. The creation of a list of contact names and numbers for all the many healthcare professionals now in your lives may be necessary so your extended family or support team knows where to find key information.
  o **What are our priorities now that illness is in our lives?** Standing your ground (so you don't wear yourselves out) requires that you know where you stand. If going to every sporting event (for adults or your children or grandchildren) was a standing commitment, you may need to check your energy levels before you assume or let others think, that such a pattern can continue without adjustment. Knowing what matters most and sharing those priorities with your loved ones can make each of the daily decisions easier to announce.
  o **What is important to keep the same?** For us, it was managing the simple pleasures at home; routines that have always given a rhythm to our daily lives. Sometimes, you

can't avoid changes to your routines, but if you can establish a sense of order and reliability in your daily life, it will help you move through the other regularly interfering issues that illness can present in your life. Both the caregiver and the one you are caring for can benefit from this kind of routine and regularity that bring a sameness and stability to everyday life.

- **How shall we vacation/travel now?** The illness may make your usual plans for summers at the cabin impossible or may make the annual Caribbean cruise illogical. The normal, ordinary patterns of life may very well be disrupted by the realities of illness in your lives. That does not mean that all fun must cease! Looking for what you can do, and what would add joy and renewal to your lives is critical. Choosing what will replenish both of you, rather than deplete you, is the key. Keeping it simpler may be more rewarding, especially if conserving energy is critical for either of you or both of you.

- **Have we talked about the funeral?** I raise this as a side-issue only because, while you can manage final arrangements at the last minute, it might prove helpful to tackle these decisions earlier, and in a more relaxed and planful conversation. If you are part of a religious tradition, broaching the subject with your clergy person may give you a whole folder of materials unique to the customs and rituals used in that religious tradition. With such tools, your family can decide together about the many decisions that go into planning a funeral service. Consider things like:
  - Do you want burial or cremation – or something else entirely?
  - Do you want a traditional funeral or a celebration of life?
  - Do you want a religious ceremony?
  - Who is the preferred presider?

- Is there meaningful music you want to be sure to include?
- Are there readings, poetry, scriptures or texts that matter to you?
- Are there distant friends who should be alerted or invited?
- Are there key elements of the eulogy you want included?
- Do you want flowers, or would you prefer gifts to a particular charity?

These and other questions that experts (funeral directors, clergy, etc.) can offer you may be helpful to you and to your family members who probably cannot guess what your individual responses would be to such questions. Writing it all down will make their work so much easier, knowing that they have a set of instructions to guide their choices, especially when emotions are predictably running high.

- **Books and resources that you may find valuable** — At the end of the book you will find all the references cited within the text, and beyond that, you will see a bibliography of books and articles that I have appreciated. Each has marked a portion of my own education as a caregiver. Many are, as you might expect, directed specifically at the needs of the dementia caregiver. Others are more generic and intended to help anyone who finds themselves in the role of a family caregiver. Please make use of this list to build your own your own collection of resources.

> Jule's experience -- *nine years ago, my elderly parents desperately needed my care and attention. They were living in the same home where they'd raised all their children, nine of us, and I moved in to tend to their increasing needs. Dad was diagnosed with Parkinson's disease and suffered the frequent falls that the condition causes. No matter where I might be, mom would call me for every spill, minor or major, and I would leave work, drop everything – I was on call 24/7. Time moved on and their needs grew exponentially. And, since I had no family of my own, my siblings relied on me. I managed everything – for a while. Then, I got sick. My diagnosis was ambiguous and my clinicians got several things wrong. As a result, I only got worse. Dad ended up in a nursing facility, because without me around, mom couldn't cope with his needs. My siblings finally realized they needed to participate, and ultimately they did. Mom now lives in an assisted living community where I can be the daughter, and others are available to address her needs for care and services. The physical and emotional consequences were, for me, life-altering. I'm still just recovering. But the experience taught me to first care for myself and then, contribute to the care of others, even those I love.*

This this whole book is built on the premise that you are caring for someone who is on a path of declining health, logically ending in their death. While this may not be the exact scenario for every reader, we all die, and the one you are caring for will not escape that ending, whether it comes as a result of the disease, condition or illness that currently requires your care or not.

I did not write this section on the assumption that I know the future – I surely do not – but all too often, when we find ourselves in the role of family caregiver, we feel too overwhelmed to look very far ahead. We are so caught up in the needs and the work of the present that we cannot imagine what we will need to know or understand even more than we do today. This book serves as a way of helping you see that some diseases do have a predictable, if not precise, trajectory, and if you are prepared for the whole journey, you will be able to endure each part with more confidence. What I've included here are some arenas of learning that are important for you to consider.

Chapter Four
Self-care Strategies for your Spiritual Needs

Spirituality is an all-encompassing topic, yet strangely enough it is all too often excluded when we think about our self-care needs. Frequently it is confused with religious pursuits or practices which, for some people may be a significant part of their way of addressing things related to the "spirit", but religion is not the only way we access care for ourselves and our spiritual needs.

What does a spiritual need look like? Can you identify your spiritual needs? Sometimes they show up as emotional needs, outbursts, sadness, tears or loneliness. Sometimes they show up as physical needs, fragmented sleep, and lack of appetite, cravings or even pain. So, it can be difficult to differentiate our spiritual needs (as a category) from other kinds of needs we experience. Here is my three-question formula for knowing when a symptom (how the need shows up) is primarily spiritual:

1. **Does it gnaw at my sense of self** – does it make me question who I am, whether I'm sufficient to the tasks before me, whether I will survive the experience?
2. **Does it separate me from my sense of community** – does it make me feel isolated, disconnected, or distant from those I love and those I know care for me?

3. **Does it make me question my beliefs** – does it make me doubt what has sustained me for a lifetime, to wonder if there is any justice in the world or to ask, "Why me?"

If I can answer yes to any of these three (and certainly if I answer yes to all of them) then the need is, at its core, a spiritual need. Spiritual needs must be addressed differently than emotional needs or physical needs. They require reconnecting with our spirit, in a calm, quiet place that allows us to ask the hard questions of ourselves and find answers that are not only healing but transformative.

How do you connect with your spirit? There are many ways we do this. Each of us may have a host of ways that we make this connection. Knowing what works for you is crucial – it allows you to maintain that connection and replenish it when the road gets challenging. Some of us connect to spirit by going to a sacred space that could be a church, a temple, a mosque or even a forest or a waterfall. Not every sacred space was built by human hands. Some find sacred places out in nature, where the sacred is alive and breathing, and inviting us to do the same. Where is your sacred space? Can you create one for yourself? This could be one of the greatest gifts you give yourself – a place to be alone, connected to your spirit, a nurturing place that doesn't require you to go anywhere or do anything, but just to *be*.

I have such a place in my home. It is part office, part reading room, and mostly a sanctuary. It is where I go to read, to meditate or to just quietly pray. It has objects that I cherish and that remind me of richly spiritual events or times in my life. It has an aromatherapy diffuser that allows me to choose a fragrance (lavender for calm, citrus for wakefulness, rosemary for clarity) to suit my needs. It has a CD player that helps me choose a mood – often I choose calming, instrumental music that allows me to relax and prevents distraction often caused by lyrics. It has several lighting sources that let me invite in bright daylight or rely on low-level incandescent lamps to quiet my spirit.

What would your sanctuary, your sacred space look like? What essential elements would it contain that could immediately calm you and invite your spirit to find rest? Consider your own needs and imagine that you might create such a place for yourself to replenish your spirit. It need not be a whole room – it might be just a portion of a wall that you can gaze upon and be reminded of who you are, where you come from, what matters to you, what fills your heart with joy and where you can easily take your sorrow. It may have religious elements to it, or not. Whatever is required for you to find that space healing and even transformative – I hope you make such a place for yourself.

Spiritual needs are often neglected because we don't know how to address them. There is no one, sure-fire way to meet every spiritual need, but to neglect a spiritual need can only serve to make it deeper, wider, more of a chasm in our soul. Here are several ways you might consider addressing a need that you notice is distinctly spiritual, even though it may have either physical or emotional components or both. You might:

- Read poetry or inspiring quotes
- Read scripture or a sacred text
- Read works by an author who consistently inspires you
- Meditate
- Go on a retreat (even a mini-retreat)
- Write in a journal
- List five things each day for which you're grateful
- Get out in nature
- Listen to calming or uplifting music
- Connect with a friend who loves you
- Stretch
- Dance
- Sing
- Pray
- Practice mindfulness (focus on whatever you're doing, richly notice the details of every-day activities like washing dishes)
- Sit still
- Lie down (not with the intention of sleep, but it's okay if that happens)
- Close your eyes and invite your other senses to inform you

- Taste something lovely (a bar of chocolate you love, a coffee you enjoy, a tea you appreciate!)
- Use aromatherapy and select a fragrance that captures your attention and makes you feel good.

This is not meant to be an exhaustive list, merely a set of suggestions that I hope will inspire you to find activities you can engage in that quiet your soul, uplift your spirit, remind you that you are sacred and sufficient and that there is a larger universe of support you can call upon (whether you name that as God, or not) who can and will see you through any crisis of the spirit.

We are holistic beings. We have bodies, souls, and spirits, and in each of these parts of our whole selves, we experience needs. This is especially true when we are confronted with the pain and anguish of another, someone we love and care for. When you devote your life and your time, your energy and resources to the care of another, you will encounter your own needs that must be addressed. The responsibilities of care-giving are best performed when our own cup is full. As stated earlier, we are well-advised to follow the wisdom of the airline attendant, "Put on your own mask before attempting to assist others"; good advice for anyone trying to be a family caregiver.

In the remainder of this chapter, I will address several spiritual needs that I have commonly encountered, in myself and others. This is also not an exhaustive list, but it will set the stage for you to consider when you feel that deep, hole in your heart, that ache in your soul, that perhaps, requires your attention and is a spiritual need. Those spiritual needs that I'll address include:

- Getting Rid of Guilt
- Slogging Through Anguish
- Examining the Existential
- Feeling Forsaken

- **Getting Rid of Guilt** – Guilt is what we feel when we judge our actions to have fallen short of our own expectations. Other people can "guilt you", but you don't need to pick it up. I had a mother who was very good at "guilting" others as a form of manipulation. She would want me (or whomever she was guilting) to feel ashamed of not meeting her expectations, and thus, feel guilty. The dilemma about guilt is that most of the time, we do it to ourselves; *we guilt ourselves*. Have you heard yourself say (or think) anything like this?

- "He made me promise never to put him in a facility!"
- "It's her birthday, and I'm not able to go be with her!"
- "All he wanted was for me to sit a little while longer, but I had to go!"
- "My kids need this my husband needs that; everyone expects me to be there for them!"
- "What if she dies and I'm not beside her?"
- "What if he falls and I'm not around?"

These are all questions and statements made to order up a dose of guilt. Right behind each question, you could hear that inner voice say, *"I really should..."* our internal voices that bring up the *"shoulds," "oughts,"* and *"musts"* of life that are there to conjure up guilt, and often in multiple servings. Why do this to yourself, when there is probably some friend or family member who will do it for you (but only if you let them)?

Guilt is a useless feeling except when you honestly owe someone an apology for disregarding their request or failing to keep a promise. There are situations when we should feel guilty. Consider these:

- I would rightfully feel guilty if I played hooky from school or work because the weather was so delightful that I just wanted to play.
- I would rightfully feel guilty if I had all weekend to do a chore a dear friend asked of me and I simply chose not to even try to do it.
- I would rightfully feel guilty if I went out with friends instead of spending the evening with my spouse on our anniversary.

For actions such as these, I should offer my honest and sincere apology.

It is neither helpful nor healthy to feel guilty simply because we're carrying around too much responsibility for the happiness of others. Especially when as family caregivers, we have to reach a balance point where we can say, "I've done my best!" and be able to have compassion on ourselves, like we would on any other human.

Guilt grips us into spending sleepless nights worrying about things we cannot change or fix. Guilt storms around in the back of our brains nagging at us that we could have done more, we could have made the event better, we could have outdone ourselves, exhausted ourselves to please our incessant sense of guilt that we have never done or been enough.

If no one has said it to you lately, or worse, if no one has ever said it to you at all, allow me the honor of telling you:

> YOU ARE ENOUGH!

You have done enough, said enough, bent over backward enough! You have done your very best and that is all that anyone (including yourself) can ask of you. **You've got enough! You do enough! And it is remarkable how "enough" you really are!**

Please take these words to heart! Guilt is your own worst enemy because it will cloud your judgment and make you believe that you could be better than your best, if only you tried harder. That is the kind of thinking that will make you lose sight of all the positive things you've accomplished, all the kindnesses you've shown and all the extra miles you've already gone.

In considering my situation caring for my husband, I made a list that allowed me to set down my guilt and acknowledge that all was sufficiently well in our lives, given the over-arching circumstances of his illness. Here's my list that represents key elements of quality of life (for now), he is:

- Clean enough
- Fed enough
- Hydrated enough
- Medicated enough
- Entertained enough
- Free to move around (within logical safety limits)
- Welcome to express his opinion (even if angry)
- With companions (me or others) enough for stimulation
- Receiving kisses daily
- Offered ice cream -- liberally, and whenever requested
- Able to access cookies (as long as I don't need to bake)
- Dragged to only minimal medical visits
- Represented (by his wishes) in formal DNR/DNI and POLST documents.

For me, this is my list of enough. It is what keeps me from blaming myself when life happens and things don't go as well as I'd prefer. No one can lift guilt off of you; you have to give it up yourself. You have to shed it like a heavy backpack and leave it by the side of the road if you want to complete the journey with your soul and spirit intact.

- **Slogging Through Anguish** – What I mean by anguish, is that sense of severe mental or physical pain or suffering that is often self-imposed or accompanies an unimaginably difficult decision. As family caregivers, we are necessarily charged with making decisions for and about those in our care. Some of those decisions seem impossible to make. They tear at our hearts, they make us question whether we've done all we can, considered all the options and are choosing what is truly in the best interest of the person in our care. We often describe our anguish with terms like agony, pain, torment, torture, distress, angst, misery, sorrow, grief, heartache, heartbreak, unhappiness, woe, desolation or even despair. It is an awful place to find ourselves and, unfortunately, no one can get us out of anguish except ourselves – it is a spiritual problem (need) and requires a spiritual response, which only the one with the need can pursue. No one else can heal your spirit, it has to come from you.

Anguish often comes when it is time to end physical life; when you're asked to end a life by pulling the plug on their life support systems in their last days or moments. You're authorized to be the decision-maker, but that does not necessarily make the decision itself any easier. You may know their wishes and even have those wishes documented and notarized, but in the moment of decision, the experience is often anguishing. We are caught up with all the "what if" questions – they generally lead us to inevitable pain because no one knows the answers to those questions, if they did, the decision would be clearer, easier to make.

Anguish may come from the exhaustion of caring for a loved one on a predictably deteriorating trajectory. You know where it is it taking you and the one in your care, you wish it were not the case, but it is. The end-point is inevitable, albeit imprecise. We may not know when the end will come or even the next benchmark that reminds us of the end, but we know it is coming and we are left to watch and wait. The waiting alone can be anguishing, and often we may be alone in our waiting, if there is no one there to support, encourage or sustain us in that seemingly endless effort.

How do you deal with anguish? For most of us, finding a safe place to cry or even to wail may be the first solution. To visibly and viscerally cry out in our pain and let the heavens know how deeply we feel this suffering. While that does not remove the anguish, it may relieve the stress, albeit temporarily.

My "go-to" place to take my anguish has always been the shower. It has served as a safe place to cry, to weep, to complain and to pound my fists where no one would hear me, except the heavens. It may be of benefit to find your own place where you can safely go to cry and let out the anguish that can surely overtake you as a caregiver. Your place may be in the loving arms of a person who knows and cares for you, who can see you and your pain and not be overwhelmed by either. I would urge you to find such a place (one or more) where you can turn in times of such deep pain in life.

Anguish can also come from circumstances of neglect. Sometimes we wait too long to say what needs to be said, to forgive, to speak our love out-loud, to ask for someone's pardon or to allow our heart to emerge with plain, bold language. That missed opportunity can produce its own anguish when the time has passed for such disclosures to be made. If we wait too long to speak from our heart we may miss the opportunity to be forgiven, to be acknowledged, to be witness to deep endearment or to have our love richly requited. It is up to us, even though we may wish to make it someone else's responsibility, to speak our truth and to do it in a timely way so that we are not left with the anguish of neglect.

The remedies for anguish are to acknowledge it when it arises, give it voice and volume if needed, and then to realize that like guilt, it is a feeling we can either amplify or quiet for ourselves. We amplify it by making matters worse – by "awfulizing" and "catastrophizing" in our heads about the many ways the situation is completely intolerable. Rarely is our thinking clear or accurate when we are in anguish. So, to dwell unnecessarily on how bad it might become is truly pointless and to no one's benefit. The way we quiet anguish is the way we deal with any spiritual need. The list offered earlier in this chapter may afford you some options that can comfort you, even in the midst of anguish.

For me, if the anguish comes in a hospital, finding the chapel has served to soothe my spirit. If the anguish comes at home, to just go outside and look at nature, listen to the birds, the wind, the rustle of the leaves – these things can soothe my anguish. I cannot speak for you, but I would urge you to acknowledge your times of anguish, to share them with someone you trust, if that is an option for you. To choose meaningful ways to calm and quiet your spirit to acknowledge that the anguish you are experiencing is a deep and common experience for any family caregiver.

- **Examining the Existential** – This is what we do when we ask ourselves, "Why me?" Or, when we're concerned for our loved-one, "Why him?" or "Why her?" as if there was any logical explanation. What we're really asking is not, why did this happen to us, but why do bad things happen to good people? This is in part the title of a marvelous book I'd recommend to you, if you have not already read it, *When Bad Things Happen to Good People*, by Harold S. Kushner (2007). In his book, Rabbi Kushner explains several key truths:

- o If we could only make sense of innocent people suffering then we could live with it, or manage it, or rationalize it. We can't of course, but we think this reasoning makes sense when we're confronted with what seems like an injustice.
- o Heartache, tragedy, loss, and pain are human experiences that help us recognize and appreciate what is good in the world by simple contrast. Such events help us gain perspective on good versus evil, what is right versus wrong, and enable us to determine what sort of people we want to be or become.
- o Life's challenges strengthen us and give us good reason to be of service to each other.

So, what does your existential crisis sound like?

In our house, it may start with my husband saying, "You don't deserve this!" He means to comfort me with these words, but they bring no comfort. To say that I don't deserve this (the responsibility of caring for him through his illness), is to suggest that someone does. The greater truth is, NO ONE DESERVES THIS. But, life isn't about just desserts. It is about the well-distributed difficulties we humans encounter; everyone's got their troubles. These just happen to be ours.

When we fail to see that the challenges we encounter are just that; our challenges, and not a road-block on the pathway to our special and protected lives, we've made the first step in moving forward. Each life is as "special" as the next. None of us is entitled to a life without upset, crisis, tragedy or trial. Some lives are dealt more blows than others. When you notice that there are lives equally challenging as your own, you are beginning to gain perspective.

Yes, we all encounter troubles. Family caregivers often encounter them in spades. But to sulk in the notion that your suffering will be relieved if you can just figure out why it happened is folly. Likewise, to imagine that there is some deep wisdom to be found in figuring out who's got the worse situation, is a waste of valuable time. We all have troubles. Let's figure out how to help each other through the chaos we call life. Why we live, why we die – that's just the human condition. How we live and how we die – those are questions worth asking. Looking for the choices we can make along the way is what matters in the end:

- o Who can I befriend – whose troubles can I understand?
- o Who can I support – because I've walked the path they're on?
- o Where can I turn for help – because my load feels heavy today?
- o What can I learn from this situation? What's the life-lesson here?

These are the questions that help us examine the existential nature of illness, our own or someone else's.

- **Feeling Forsaken** – To feel forsaken is to feel utterly alone, abandoned, deserted. When someone we love, especially a partner, someone we've depended upon, made plans with, or shared life's load falls ill, we do feel left alone. Where there once were two – there is now one person to:
  - o Tend to all the household chores,
  - o Figure out the solution to daily difficulties,
  - o To manage all life's details.

It is easy to feel sorry for yourself under such circumstances but, to let that go on for days is not a productive use of anyone's time and energy!

Mostly we feel the sharp pain of change. It used to be that we had help, now it feels like we're going it alone. We've been forsaken.

But it isn't just that – it is the sense that we've been caught off guard, surprised by this whole sad trick. It is the belief (a very limiting belief) that this wasn't supposed to happen; but, it did! The key is to get past the belief that's limiting your forward motion and get on with what you must do, care for your loved one and yourself. Here's how it sounds inside our heads:

- o How can this be, they were so healthy, so strong?
- o What could have prevented this, did I (we) do something wrong?
- o Life was going so well. We were right on track with our plans!

None of us is promised a life without pain, without challenge or hardship. What we do with the trials we're handed is the key to how well we (and all those who depend on us) will fare going forward. This means we have choices – every step of the way. We have choices even when we don't think we do. This is especially true even when it feels like there isn't a choice, as if it is all in fate's hands.

What are the choices you're facing? Here are some of the choices I recognize within my life, maybe they will sound familiar to you:

- o How can I do this?
- o Who can help me find my way through?
- o What will happen next?
- o How can I prepare for whatever's coming?
- o Who can I add to my team with this skill-set?
- o Why is this so hard!?

The choice we must make about seeking help is not so much as to whether we'll seek help, but from whom. The choice is to stop hiding behind our needs and turn to others who can (and very often will) help us through the current difficulty.

Chapter Five

Self-care Strategies for Getting through Grief

You may find yourself in grief when you least expect it. Being a caregiver can bring you, and the person in your care, wave after wave of loss, large and small. With each of these losses, depending upon the importance each one represents in your lives, there may be a logical and fully appropriate grief response. Unfortunately, these can come in rapid succession, like a storm of losses. And before you know it, you slip into deep in grief – in a place of sadness where you never expected to be.

So, let's consider all these losses, all these opportunities for grief, within the context of the work of a well-known writer on grief, Elisabeth Kübler-Ross, the Swiss-American psychiatrist who wrote, On Death and Dying (1973) and gave us languages for the stages of grief:

1. **Denial** – In the first stage or reaction to death or loss, we are likely to think the news (the diagnosis, death or loss) is a mistake. We cling to the false reality we prefer, but which, relieves us of the thought of such separation.
2. **Anger** – This second stage is where we recognize that we cannot continue in our disbelief; it is not serving us. This is a place where we can easily cycle into those existential questions, "Why me; why us?" which can intensify our anger.

3. **Bargaining** – The third stage leads us to the hope that we can negotiate away the pain; that there is some way to stop or at least mitigate the source of our grief.
4. **Depression** – The fourth stage is where we recognize how much energy grief can take from us. We feel tired, sad and often listless. We feel depleted, we're ready to five up on ourselves, on others and on the whole situation. We might also despair at the realization that we are mortal and rather than accept that, we may become sullen, distant or seek to mourn alone. Prolonged time in depression is a danger to our own health.
5. **Acceptance** – The fifth stage helps us reach the point where we can begin to acknowledge that everything is going to be okay. We begin to reframe our understanding of the situation; we see it as real and reflective of the human condition – a condition we can now begin to embrace rather than avoid. Humans are mortal. I am human, therefore, I am mortal. Sometimes in this stage we feel a sense of calm. The loss is inevitable, but it no longer brings terror or doom. It is the stage where we can reflect on life – our own and the life of another who may be dying or already deceased.

For family caregivers, grief may come repeatedly, and that is a very normal and common experience. It can catch us off-guard. We can find ourselves in grief with any one of a number of significant losses we encounter as caregivers. Usually we will not recognize our emotional state as one of grief, but it often is. Here are some of the losses I recall in recent years while caring for my husband; each one produced a state of grief:

- When we stopped long-distance travel because airports and crowds added too much stress to the thought of a vacation;
- When we stopped going to movie theaters because the darkness or the room and its sound system startled him and would provoke terror;

- When we stopped having friends over for dinner because he could no longer manage polite conversation, even with people he'd known for years;
- When we stopped decorating the house for holidays; I realized I was the only one doing the work and the decorations brought him no joy anymore.

Your grief experiences will be your own. But whenever the realization that something important is lost, not to return, it is fair to recognize that the loss may very well bring you grief.

Our culture is not good at making room for such experiences. We are taught to dismiss them as unimportant but, that is simply not true. Each of these losses changes the rhythm of life and to deny that such alterations are important is to lie to yourself and to others. But owning it, admitting that what you're experiencing is grief, may also not be easy in today's world where the messages you're receiving from others around you tell you to suck it up and tell everyone, "I'm fine!" Sooner or later, the grief will catch up with you; you will have to admit that you are not "fine"; you are grieving.

But, you are also not flawed, damaged, sick or in an awful state. It is grief and giving it a name, recognizing it every time it visits you is critical to learning to deal with it in a healthy way. Giving grief its space, letting it wash over you, spill into tears, bring on its sadness – these are simply the most human expressions we know, especially in the face of loss. We grieve. How we relate to ourselves in suffering, how we treat ourselves in those dark hours is a crucial opportunity for applying self-care strategies. One key self-care strategy in the midst of grief is to be gentle on ourselves.

Each encounter with grief need not be as deep and lasting as a death experience, but there is no one who can tell you the timetable on which your feelings will operate. Emotions do not run on schedule and they will wash over us when we least expect them. In grief, we owe it to ourselves to be as gracious and kind to our own spirit as we would be with a dear friend. How would we speak to a friend in grief? Hopefully we would offer words of care, of concern and compassion. Hopefully we would speak kindly and with generosity of spirit; with understanding and with calm.

If you are someone who generally speaks to yourself harshly, if you are often self-critical, mean-spirited or derogatory in the language you use toward yourself, I invite you to change your ways. Self-care often begins with self-talk. Learning to speak gently and with kindness to ourselves, rather than to criticize or deride ourselves, is key to softening into a place of forgiveness and comfort. While we may encounter a harsh world outside, one we cannot change, there is no need to create a harsh internal world as well – we can learn to befriend ourselves. A grief encounter is a perfect place to start.

Grief may also befall the person who is ill and the recipient of all your caregiving. We tend not to think that the person in our care may be grieving, but they may be. Each loss that the person encounters may feel like a huge defeat, and the accumulation of losses can for that person, just as for us as caregivers, bring on enormous grieving. What kinds of losses might the one in your care encounter? Consider these:

- When friends stop coming by because they just don't know what to say;
- When common joys like eating and drinking are no longer pleasant, or require assistance;
- When independence is fleeting as walking requires a cane or a walker;
- When hygiene and bathroom needs can no longer be independently managed.

Any of these, and certainly all of them taken together, could bring anyone to a place of grief. The loss of life as we've known and enjoyed is certainly something we might mourn as each change reminds us of an impending end.

With grief may also come a kind of guilt. In Chapter Four we covered guilt in some depth and I urged you then, as I do now, to get rid of unnecessary guilt. But guilt that emerges in grief may come to us as a teacher. In that case, our role is to determine what the guilt has come to teach; what are the lessons to be learned? If you think this might be where you (or the one in your care) find yourself, consider what the guilt is trying to teach. And, rather than judging the guilt, or yourself for experiencing it, imagine just sitting with it, getting to know it, learning what it has brought to you. You might ask:

- How can I learn from this guilt? What is it here to show me?
- How can I give myself permission to just sit with my guilt, become familiar with it?
- What might it be masking? (While guilt may hurt, the void of loss may hurt far more, so we find ourselves feeling guilty, rather than embracing our sadness.)
- Can I just take the time (be patient) and let myself get through this?

Again, these questions are intended as a way of inviting self-care rather than self-criticism. To encounter guilt in the midst of grief is like one who might come by an old friend and just sit with it, hold its hand, feel its familiar resonance. This may be a healthy way through both the guilt and the grief. Being patient with ourselves in every circumstance, but especially when we're in grief, is an essential path for potential growth.

Most people understand and expect that grief will come when someone we love dies. Grief may resolve smoothly or it may become complex and complicated. It can be challenging for those who experience such grief and for those around them who long to see them recover from their grief. If complex grief is not resolved, it becomes necessary to seek outside assistance from a counselor or therapist, trusted clergyperson, a social worker, psychologist as it can lead to lasting and serious consequences for the person who grieves.

Grief may very well require that you share your pain with others in order to get through the experience successfully. I've already said that complex grief – grief that is unresolved – can lead to serious consequences. There is no magic timeline for the length of your grief. There are, however, a number of studies which examine unresolved grief and its outcomes. A common milestone is two to two-and-one-half (2 – 2.5) years out from the event (a death). If we are still in the pain of Kubler-Ross's stages of anger, bargaining and depression, we are not likely to recover a sense of well-being without help.

I was recently asked what *resolved* grief looks like. I can only speak from my own experience and say, when grief has resolved, the person who was grieving is at peace. Resolution isn't closure, it isn't the end of memories or the heart-felt sentiments that linger about the person you've lost. Resolution for me, is the capacity to say to myself, *"I did all I could, I gave it my best, I will miss that person's presence in my life but, I can embrace all that we shared without remorse that it came to an end."*

While I am no expert in grief counseling, there are three kinds of grief that, I want to call out for you for further consideration if only because they can be confusing for the person who experiences them and for the people around them. This section will not offer a definitive explanation of them as each one could fill a book of its own but, may offer you enough language to describe what you're feeling, should you need to pursue professional help in addressing any of their symptoms. If grief persists, if it is complicated by years of repeated and accumulated losses, there can be a prolonged depression that persists, even well beyond the usual two-and-one-half years. The three kinds of grief are:

- Complex Grief
- Ambiguous Grief (or ambiguous loss)
- Anticipatory Grief.

Complex Grief – Is encountered as any severe, prolonged, and disabling grief reactions (Lenferink & Eisma, 2018). Such persisting symptoms of grief can clinically lead to a mental health diagnosis of "persistent complex bereavement disorder" or "prolonged grief disorder", either of which require the services of a knowledgeable psychiatric or psychologic clinician to achieve a healthy resolution.

It is messy at best to try and offer simple descriptions of these persistent and troublesome effects of grief. Even the writers who call out the complexity of diagnosing, and treating persons with such challenging disorders ask of their medical colleagues that, "further development of grief disorders within these classification systems should aim to give succinct and the least complex descriptions of symptoms or diagnostic algorithms, to be able to make useful distinctions between normal and pathological grief" (Lenferink & Eisma, 2018). It is not a simple matter to say that your grief, or anyone's grief is complex. But if you note that it is persistent and unresolved, I would urge you to seek care and treatment for yourself.

Ambiguous Grief (Loss) – Boss (2004), a seasoned researcher, notes that there is an ambiguous loss faced by the caregivers of persons with dementia. In her words, families experience ambiguous loss when they recognize "…any family member or person who is 'there, but not there.' …I have called that theoretical construct ambiguous loss" (p553). In such cases, the person "may be physically present but only a vestige of what he used to be, and even when the loss of selfhood appears irrevocable...may still vacillate between periods of lucidity where their 'former' selves resurface" (Liew, Tai, Yap & Koh, 2019). This is especially true if the person you've been caring for suffered from dementia (of any sort). This can create dreadful upset and confusion for the caregiver and other family members, which may not be fully appreciated until a much later time. Failure to recognize that this ambiguous loss is part of grief can lead to unresolved grief.

Anticipatory Grief – Is another type of unfamiliar grief and refers to the situations when we find ourselves in grief, often deeply, even before the loss has occurred. The findings of Cheung, Ho, Cheung, Lam & Tse (2018), indicate that among their 180 caregiver-subjects, "spousal caregivers caring for relatives in a later stage of dementia experienced the highest level of AG [anticipatory grief] and subjective caregiving burden, as compared with spousal caregivers caring for relatives in an earlier stage of dementia and adult children caregivers. Well-being was significantly negatively correlated with AG and subjective caregiver burden, while AG was also significantly correlated with subjective caregiver burden" (Cheung, Ho, Cheung, Lam & Tse, 2018).

In anticipatory grief, we see the one we care for losing ground, lacking energy, eating less, sleeping more and as we find ourselves anticipating that we will lose the person we love – we slip from sadness into grief. When we, as caregivers are prematurely in grief, it can wear on the very person we're taking care of. This can build a layer of sorrow and sadness between us, just at a time when we most need and want closeness and connection with the one in your care.

Anticipatory grief is hard to understand, it can be difficult to notice and before we know where our emotional energy has gone, we find ourselves in a place of grief we did not expect to experience so early in the process. It is confusing, upsetting and dangerously distancing. While not an uncommon experience, if it is not recognized and addressed, like any other grief need, lasting consequences can ensue. This is another occasion when discussing your feelings with a counselor or therapist, trusted clergy-person, a social worker or a psychologist may help you through the challenges of this experience.

Regardless of what your loved one has suffered, no matter what their illness or affliction, your own healing, your return to well-being, requires that you look after yourself throughout grief. This is true, no matter how long it takes. You cannot give up on yourself. You are absolutely worth the effort, time and attention, concern and compassion for yourself and that shared by others in order to make your way safely through the grief experience. Please, apply your best attention to caring for yourself (and inviting the care of others) when you find yourself encountering grief as a caregiver. Self-care may genuinely save your life.

One way to assist our grief toward resolution – toward acceptance and a sense of well-being – is to talk about what we're experiencing with others. Sometimes we're reluctant to do this because we don't believe others can handle what we need to say. We underestimate their capacity for understanding our pain, accepting our loss and embracing us in our sadness. We may need to express some of that anger over the death of someone we've loved deeply and given years of our life to care for. We may need to even bargain our way through the misery we're feeling or negotiate for some kind of exchange for all the effort we've put out, all the burden we've borne and all the sadness we've endured. But because such emotions may make some feel embarrassed, "I shouldn't feel this way," some are upset "No one wants to hear me rant," or some feel in the wrong, "How can I say that about someone I cared for?" we repress the need to say what is on our hearts.

Caregivers may also experience an unexpected measure of relief when the person in their care dies. This is especially true when your caregiving experience has been prolonged and difficult. It is very common to have a sense of relief that this portion of your life is finished and you will not be witnessing the suffering of someone you care for on a daily basis anymore. It is a normal feeling, and not something to feel guilty over. The relief that some caregivers experience or even anticipate, and the guilt associated with feeling that sense of relief is a common and natural set of feelings. There is nothing wrong with feeling either the relief or the guilt. They are simply feelings. Acknowledge them and give them space.

I am here to tell you, there is no shame in what you're feeling – no matter what it is, how awful it feels, how dreadful your words may sound in your own head! There is no shame in grieving. We have to let it out. We have to find a safe place to say the words, think the thoughts, express the feelings and realize that they represent ordinary human emotions. We are not a "bad person" because our thoughts and words and feelings are not pleasant to hear. They are ours, we need to own them and give them a voice. Feelings of any kind bottled up inside cannot find healing. It has been said, "The only way out is *through!*" This is the journey through grief.

Where can you speak your heart? I can offer some suggestions:

- Call or visit a close, trusted friend
- Contact clergy (a chaplain, priest, rabbi, pastor, etc.)
- See a counselor (many varieties from psychologist to other therapists)
- Join a support-group (specifically a support-group for those in grief may help).

There is no "one way" through. Your way, your path, through grief will be your own. You may need one person to talk with or you may need several – there is no right or wrong way to heal. The only danger is to avoid healing.

Epilogue

Your Story

Somewhere between your "worst day on Earth" and your "happiest memories" there is a truthful story about your experience as a family caregiver. I can say that truthfully because there is also *the story we tell ourselves.* That story may not exactly be the whole truth, but it is what we reinforce in our minds by saying it over and over to ourselves, and to others who are willing to listen.

Sometimes *the story we tell ourselves* needs or deserves an editor. I say this because, in writing this book I've been helped tremendously by the editorial comments of trusted friends who read it before publication and an actual editor who cleaned up my grammar and syntax. We all need editors in our life and in our consciousness. Without that inner-editor words slip out sideways and we find ourselves asking, "Did I say that out loud?"

For your story, I wish you the time to think about all you want and need to say.

Sometimes what we repeatedly say (to ourselves and to others) is not what we mean to say, not what we want to say, not what we are well-served by saying. Here's what I mean by that; sometimes what we say (over and over) reinforces a belief in us that becomes (seemingly) insurmountable, and it is not. It is just that, a belief, something we've adopted as an explanation for how we live our lives and, usually because it served a purpose when we created it. However, as you look back on *the story you tell yourself*, I urge you to ask yourself, "Is this the story I want to go on hearing in my head or saying in my conversations"?

I do not wish to make your story wrong. I do not wish to make your story different, unless your story no longer serves you, no longer brings you what you need to hear or say. Let me explain. *The story we tell ourselves should serve us*; it should feed the best that is in us, inspire us toward our most heart-felt work, and should satisfy our soul in its telling and hearing. I've used that word *should* here because, the story we tell ourselves is our own and if there is a 'should' worth remembering it is that our story can and should serve us well.

The story we tell ourselves can morph and change over time. It can become richer and fuller, more or less detailed. It can be longer or shorter, softer or harsher. But, whatever we put into *the story we tell ourselves* it should serve us well. What I mean by that is the language we choose, the phrases we repeat, the message we send (to ourselves and to others) can reinforce our best intentions, remind us of the greatness we carry inside us, uplift the listener and inspire us (and others) to action.

Good stories do all that. Good stories serve us. They bring about a greater good than the events they describe or highlight. I want you to make your story, *the story you tell yourself,* a GREAT story. But, you will ask, "How can I make my story great? It is what it is!" And, I would agree that for the moment, that is true but, I would ask, "Does it serve you well?" When others hear you tell your story is it. . .

- Full of complaint and sadness?
- Cluttered with blame for others?
- Enmeshed in *if only* or other regrets?
- Wrapped up in woes?

Have you constructed your story to reinforce for yourself, and anyone who will listen, how awful life is, how dreadful your plight, how deep your sacrifice or how endless your service to the one in your care? If so, please trust me, your story, *the story you keep telling yourself* isn't serving you well.

As caregivers, our stories have sadness. They have grief and sorrow, anguish and frustration, fear and loneliness and often death and dying. Those are all elements of human truth. But our story, *the story we tell ourselves*, must also have elements of joy, happiness, redemption and inspiration, if we are to grow and to learn, teach and uplift with our story. Even if the ones we uplift are ourselves.

So, I ask you again, D*oes Your Story Serve You Well?* And, if not, are you ready to rewrite your story? This means more than just changing the language you use; it means changing your approach to how you live your life. It means looking deep within and telling the whole truth about the choices you've made, the values that matter and the hopes and hurts you hold dear.

You can take a story that does not serve you well and transform it into one that will by simply examining your opportunities for change, in both language and action. Consider a story:

- Full of complaint and sadness – can you see yourself reaching out for help and being able to add the banquet of bounty that others bring to you as part of your new story?
- Cluttered with blame for others – can you imagine yourself forgiving those people for merely being themselves and failing to notice your needs?
- Enmeshed in *if only* or other regrets – can you allow yourself to move beyond those self-criticisms and say to yourself (and to others) that you took the best course of action available at the time, and that you too, deserve (self) compassion and kindness?
- Wrapped up in woes – can you find gratitude, even in sadness, and begin to notice how you have grown and changed as a result of your experiences and even your hardships?

I do not want you to put on rose-colored glasses and pretend that life is something it is not, nor deny the difficult truths of your story. But, I do invite you reconsider the value those tragic elements add to your life and the story you use to explain it. In any story, the facts do not change, but the way in which they are told, can. The facts can serve the tale they tell; this is what makes up the plot. You have the power to change the plot of your story without altering the facts at all.

I trust you will take all the time you need to consider your story and make the *story you tell yourself* a story of joy, of warmth and a story that inspires you to be and become your very best self.

NOTES

NOTES

NOTES

References

1. Acton, Gayle. *Health-promoting self-care in family caregivers.* Western Journal of Nursing Research, vol. 24 no. 1, pp. 73-86, 2002.
2. Agency for Healthcare Research and Quality, *Next Steps after your Diagnosis: Finding Information and Support,* 2005. https://www.ahrq.gov/sites/default/files/publications2/files/diaginfo.pdf.
3. Alzheimer's Association, *End-of-Life Decisions: Honoring the Wishes of a Person with Alzheimer's Disease,* 2016. https://www.alz.org/national/documents/brochure_endoflifedecisions.pdf
4. Bailey, Melissa and Aleccia, JoNel. *AARP Health Conditions and Treatments: Barbara Bush's End-Of-Life Decision Stirs Debate Over 'Comfort Care'"* Kaiser Health News, 2018. https://www.aarp.org/health/conditions-treatments/info-2018/barbara-bush-comfort-care.html
5. Boss, Pauline. *"Ambiguous loss research, theory, and practice: Reflections after 9/11."* Journal of Marriage and Family, vol. 66 no. 3, 2004, pp. 551-566, 2004
6. Brown, Brené. *"Shame and Vulnerability,"* TED Talk, 2010. https://www.ted.com/talks/brene_brown_on_vulnerability/up-next
7. Cheung, Daphne Sze Ki, et al. *"Anticipatory grief of spousal and adult children caregivers of people with dementia."* BMC Palliative Care, vol. 17 no.1, 2018, pp. 124.

8. Collins, Lauren and Swartz, Kristine. *Caregiver Care.* American Family Physician, vol. 83, no. 11, pp. 1309, 2011.
9. Crosby, Henry, Robinson, Smokey, and Wonder, Stevie. *Tears of a Clown*, 1967. Recorded by Smoky Robinson and the Miracles.
10. Deeken, John, et al. *Care for the Caregivers: a review of self-report instruments developed to measure the burden, needs, and quality of life of informal caregivers.* Journal of Pain and Symptom Management, vol. 26. no. 4, pp. 922-953, 2003.
11. Dionne-Odom, Jodie, et al. *The Self-care Practices of Family Caregivers of Persons with Poor Prognosis Cancer: Differences by varying levels of caregiver well-being and preparedness.* Supportive Care in Cancer, vol. 25, no. 8, pp. 2437-2444, 2017.
12. Donelan, K., et al. *Challenged to Care: Informal Caregivers in a Changing Health System.* Health Affairs, vol. 21, no. 4, pp. 222 – 231, 2002.
13. Family Caregiver Alliance and AARP. *Caregiver Statistics,* 2015 https://www.caregiver.org/caregiver-statistics-demographics
14. Feinberg, Lynn, et al. *Valuing the Invaluable: 2011 update, the growing contributions and costs of family caregiving.* AARP Public Policy Institute, vol. 32. Washington, DC, 2011.
15. Gaugler, Joseph E., et al. "Caregivers dying before care recipients with dementia." *Alzheimer's & Dementia: Translational Research & Clinical Interventions* 4 (2018): 688-693.
16. Kübler-Ross, Elizabeth. *On Death and Dying.* 1973, Routledge.
17. Kushner, Harold. *"When Bad Things Happen to Good People.* 2007, Anchor.
18. Lenferink, Lonneke, and Maarten Eisma. *37,650 Ways to Have 'Persistent Complex Bereavement Disorder' yet only 48 ways to have 'prolonged grief disorder.'* Psychiatry Research, vol. 261, pp. 88-89, 2018.
19. Liew, Tau Ming, et al. *Comparing the Effects of Grief and Burden on Caregiver Depression in Dementia Caregiving: a longitudinal path analysis over 2.5 years.* Journal of the American Medical Directors Association, 2019.

20. Maslow, Abraham. *A Theory of Human Motivation.* Psychological Review. vol. 50, no. 4, pp. 370–96, 1943. http://downloads.joomlacode.org/trackeritem/5/8/7/58799/AbrahamH.Maslow-ATheoryOfHumanMotivation.pdf
21. National Sleep Foundation. *Napping.* 2019. https://sleepfoundation.org/sleep-topics/napping
22. Wittenberg, Eve, and Prosser, Lisa. *Health as a Family Affair.* New England Journal of Medicine. vol. 374, no.19, pp.1804 -1806, 2016.

Bibliography & Resources

Here I've listed some of the tools and resources I've appreciated over time. It is not a definitive list of everything you might want or need but, it enough to get you started in a direction that can prove helpful. Please consult my website www.cocreate4life.com to discover an ever-growing list of resources for caregivers.

- Taylor, Richard. *Alzheimer's from the Inside Out.* Health Professions Press Baltimore, MD, 2007.
- Brown, Brené. I Thought It Was Just Me (But It Isn't): Making the Journey from What Will People Think? to I Am Enough. Avery, 2008.
- Brown, Brené. Daring greatly: How the courage to be vulnerable transforms the way we live, love, parent, and lead. Penguin, 2015.
- Brown, Brené. Braving the wilderness: The quest for true belonging and the courage to stand alone. Random House, 2017.
- Carter, Rosalynn and Golant Susan. *Helping yourself help others: A book for caregivers.* Public Affairs, 2013.
- Carter, Rosalynn. *And Thou Shalt Honor: The Caregiver's Companion.* Rodale, 2003.
- Comer, Meryl. *Slow Dancing with a Stranger: Lost and Found in the Age of Alzheimer's.* HarperOne, 2014.

- Kushner, Harold. *When Bad Things Happen to Good People.* Anchor, 2007.
- Sheehy, Gail. *Passages in Caregiving: Turning Chaos into Confidence.* HarperCollins, New York, 2010.
- Mace, Nancy and Rabins, Peter. *The 36-hour Day: A Family Guide to Caring for People who have Alzheimer's Disease, Related Dementias, and Memory Loss.* Johns Hopkins University Press, 2011.
- Snyder, Lisa. *Speaking our Minds: Personal Reflections from Individuals with Alzheimer's.* Times Books, 2000.
- Reinhard, Susan, et al. *Home Alone: Family Caregivers Providing Complex Chronic Care.* AARP Public Policy Institute, Washington, DC, 2012.
- Donelan, K., et al. *Challenged to Care: Informal Caregivers in a Changing Health System.* Health Affairs, 2002.
- Gaugler, Joseph E., et al. *Caregivers dying before care recipients with dementia.* Alzheimer's & Dementia: Translational Research & Clinical Interventions 4, 2018.
- AHRQ. *Next Steps after your Diagnosis: Finding Information and Support. Agency for Healthcare Research and Quality*, 2005. https://www.ahrq.gov/sites/default/files/publications2/files/diaginfo.pdf.
- Bailey, Melissa, and Aleccia, JoNel. *AARP Health Conditions and Treatments: Barbara Bush's End-Of-Life Decision Stirs Debate Over 'Comfort Care'* Kaiser Health News, 2018. https://www.aarp.org/health/conditions-treatments/info-2018/barbara-bush-comfort-care.html